ANTONIO MACHADO

By CARL W. COBB

Antonio Machado, although born in 1875, as poet and thinker still speaks to us in a contemporary voice. He began as a Symbolist and ended as an Existentialist, but he preferred to call himself a temporal poet. By this phrase, he meant a poet who explores the depths of his consciousness and records in his poetry the intuitions of his own lived experience, simple perhaps but unique. His preoccupation with time and memory and his anguish concerning man's future both now and hereafter make his themes still relevant in the 1970's. Moreover, as a prose writer, his invention of the Apocryphal Professor Juan de Mairena, an unsalaried professor teaching unscheduled classes outside the Establishment, was a prophetic insight. In important ways like our Robert Frost, Antonio Machado has continued to live as the poet of the Castilian land and people and as a human being of persistently tragic outlook who nevertheless exemplifies man's indomitable spirit.

TWAYNE'S WORLD AUTHORS SERIES (TWAS)

The purpose of TWAS is to survey the major writers—novelists, dramatists, historians, poets, philosophers, and critics—of the nations of the world. Among the national literatures covered are those of Australia, Canada, China, Eastern Europe, France, Germany, Greece, India, Italy, Japan, Latin America, New Zealand, Poland, Russia, Scandinavia, Spain, and the African nations, as well as Hebrew, Yiddish, and Latin Classical literatures. This survey is complemented by Twayne's United States Authors Series and English Authors Series.

The intent of each volume in these series is to present a critical analytical study of the works of the writer; to include biographical and historical material that may be necessary for understanding, appreciation, and critical appraisal of the writer; and to present all material in clear, concise English—but not to vitiate the scholarly content of the work by doing so.

Antonio Machado

By CARL W. COBB

University of Tennessee

ABOUT THE AUTHOR

Carl W. Cobb, after receiving two degrees from Peabody College, took his doctorate at Tulane University in 1961. He also studied at the Universidad Nacional in Colombia and spent the Summer of 1968 in Spain, doing research and visiting the places where Machado lived. In addition to publishing articles in the *Philological Quarterly*, the *Kentucky Foreign Language Quarterly* and other journals, he is the author of the Twayne World Authors Series volume on Federico García Lorca. At present, Dr. Cobb is an Associate Professor of Spanish at the University of Tennessee in Knoxville.

For my daughters,

Karen and Carolyn,

the one dark, the other fair.

Acknowledgments

I gratefully acknowledge the permission of Doña Matea M. de
Machado, holder of the copyright, to quote from Machado's
poetry, especially extensive sections from the following poems:
XI, XIII, XXXII, LXXIX, and CLXVII.

I am indebted to the Graduate School of the University of
Tennessee for the Summer Grant which made it possible for me
to visit the cities in which Machado lived.

Finally, I am deeply grateful to my colleague Yulan M.
Washburn and to my wife Jane for their help with the manuscript.

Preface

ANTONIO MACHADO and his poetry as a subject for study we have found to be both a blessing and a keen challenge. As a man, during his lifetime and after his death, Machado has had unqualified esteem and respect; no one has questioned the poet's own conclusion in a self-portrait that he was "in the finest sense of the word, good." His fellow writers—Unamuno, Pío Baroja, Ortega y Gasset, García Lorca—often aroused and even provoked bitter controversy. Yet even they were unanimous in their respect for and appreciation of the quiet Don Antonio, who even managed to live through a potentially dangerous autumnal romantic episode without besmirching his reputation. Thus far biographical material on him has been brief and bland, as he himself wished it; he preferred in fact, in his sly and ironic way, to reveal as much of his personality as he cared to in his own writings.

In much of his poetry Antonio Machado was a "simple" poet, with, however, all the difficulties this term implies for the critic. As someone has said, the "difficult" poets, such as the Baroque Góngora or the ultramodern García Lorca, are easy to comment upon, for deciphering the complex meanings and illustrating the elaborate forms provide continued interest. But Machado, like our own Robert Frost, utilized repetitively a few common symbols in simple traditional forms, in lyrics of little surface brilliance. As we have continued to read these lyrics over the years, however, we have felt the same deep human response which Dámaso Alonso and others have attempted to describe. Yet we have remained somewhat baffled as to how Antonio Machado achieved these effects. Therefore the problems of presenting these poems adequately even in the original are formidable, and are, of course, compounded when we must depend upon translation.

In translation, Machado offers almost insuperable difficulties for more than one reason. Much of his poetry in the symbolist manner is cast in a short lyric of brief lines and in traditional form with rhyme or Spanish assonance. The effects of the form, while simple, are of course essential, and any free rendering or substitution of symbol tends to betray the translation. Willis Barnstone, in his *Eighty Poems of Antonio Machado*, was the first to translate the poet to English, but his versions are essentially formless and therefore often disappointing. Alice Jane McVan, in her *Antonio Machado*, has included many translations in which she and her colleagues observe the form of the originals but with some clumsiness of syntax which is pseudopoetic. We have preferred to utilize our own translations, with the usual sincere apologies for their shortcomings.

Since the death of Antonio Machado almost thirty years ago, a great number of articles, monographs, and books have explored his life and work with increasing thoroughness. Still, the only book-length biography is Miguel Pérez Ferrero's *Vida de Antonio Machado y Manuel* (*Life of Antonio Machado and Manuel*), which contains many essential details but which is woefully inadequate in certain areas. The books and articles on specific periods in the poet's work have made it increasingly evident that Machado produced a significant body of poetry in three fairly distinct periods: the introspective, symbolist poetry of *Solitudes*; the objective, Generation of 1898 poetry of *Land of Castile*; and the metaphysical poetry of the *Apocryphal Songbook* during his later years. The short volumes of J. B. Trend and Allison Peers, written just after the Spanish Civil War, tended to overemphasize the Castilian period, partly because of its political overtones. Afterward critics such as Dámaso Alonso and Ricardo Gullón have convincingly stressed the intimacy of the symbolist poetry. Recently, Pablo de A. Cobos has projected the importance of the metaphysical period. Moreover, recent studies have indicated the artistic value of Machado's prose work, *Juan de Mairena*, irrespective of the originality of its philosophical ideas. Machado's philosophical ideas have been definitively studied by Antonio Sánchez Barbudo, a very competent and thorough scholar. Moreover, recently Sánchez Barbudo, in a massive *Los poemas de Antonio Machado*, has presented an organized discussion in great detail of Machado's poems one by one.

Certainly the increasing body of critical work has gradually revealed the complexity of Antonio Machado's fine mind and his literary talent of consistently high quality, with little of the immature or the occasional in his concentrated literary output. Surprisingly, thus far there has appeared no adequate comprehensive book which embraces Machado's life and emphasizes the three periods of his work, and we have set ourselves this challenging task in writing this Twayne book.

CARL W. COBB

Knoxville, Tennessee

Contents

Chapter

Preface

Chronology

1. Life and Times of Antonio Machado   17

2. The Poet and the Inner World: *Soledades*
    (*Solitudes*)   43

3. The Poet Looks Outward: *Campos de Castilla*
    (*Fields of Castile*)   76

4. The Poet as Metaphysician   104

5. Philosophy in the Service of Man:
    Juan de Mairena   128

6. The Experiment in Theater   145

7. Machado's Position and Influence   164

Notes and References   175

Selected Bibliography   181

Index   185

Chronology

1875 July 26: Antonio Machado Ruiz born in the Palacio de las Dueñas in Seville.

1883 Family moves to Madrid when his grandfather is named professor there. Antonio and his brother Manuel enrolled in the Free Institute.

1893 With the pseudonym "Longhair" Antonio publishes a series of humorous articles in *La Caricatura.*

1899 Goes to Paris with Manuel to work for the Garnier publishing house.

1902 Publishes his first book of poetry, *Soledades* (*Solitudes*), dated as of 1903.

1904 Publishes poetry in Juan Ramón Jiménez' important journal *Helios.*

1906 Begins to prepare himself for the examinations to become a teacher of French.

1907 Goes up to Soria, a provincial town in Castile, as a professor in the Secondary Institute. Second edition of *Solitudes* appears.

1909 Marries Leonor Izquierdo, a young provincial lass, in Soria.

1911 Returns to Paris on a fellowship with Leonor, who becomes seriously ill there.

1912 Publishes *Campos de Castilla* (*Fields of Castile*). Leonor dies. Machado transfers to the Institute in Baeza in Andalusia.

1917 Publishes *Páginas escogidas* (*Selected Poems*) and *Poesías completas* (*Complete Poems*).

1919 Transfers to the Institute in Segovia, where he will live until 1931.

1924 Publishes *Nuevas canciones* (*New Songs*).

1926   Publishes first part of *De un cancionero apócrifo* (*From an Apocryphal Songbook*). Apparently meets Guiomar. His añd Manuel's first play premiered in Madrid.

1931   Transfers to the Institute Calderón de la Barca in Madrid when the Second Republic is proclaimed.

1934   Publishes first parts of *Juan de Mairena* series (to appear in book form in 1936).

1936   Civil War breaks out. Antonio and his family transferred to Valencia with the Government of the Republicans.

1937   Publishes articles on the War in *Hora de España.*

1938   Transfers to Barcelona with the War going badly for the Republican cause.

1939   February 22: Antonio dies in exile in Collioure, along the border in France and is buried there. His mother dies a few days later.

1941   The Machados' last drama, *El hombre que murió en la guerra* (*The Man Who Died in the War*), staged in Madrid.

1949   Homage to Machado in *Cuadernos hispanoamericanos* and *Revista hispánica moderna.*

1959   Various expressions of homage in Collioure, the Sorbonne, Segovia, Madrid; and in many journals such as *Insula.*

CHAPTER 1

Life and Times of Antonio Machado

I *The Historical and Cultural Background*

T HE LAST quarter of the 19th century was a time of continuing political, cultural, and intellectual ferment in
Spain.[1] After the brief experiment of the First Republic in
1873, the monarchy was restored a year later, the Bourbon Al-
phonso XII ascending to the throne. The period following, now
generally called the Restoration, seemed to be one of stability
and promise. But Machado's own generation has described the
atmosphere as "carnival," meaning that the activities were often
false, the stability an illusion. The century-old struggles between
the conservative and liberal factions continued to worsen. Even-
tually the ideas of Socialism, Marxism, and Anarchism began to
filter into Spain. The brief but disastrous Spanish-American War
of 1898, brought about by the difficult problem with Cuba,
clearly indicated Spain's decline as a world power.

During this period, the cultural struggle between the conservative group, which sought to preserve Spain as she was, and the
liberal, which strove to "Europeanize" the country, continued
with intensity, and of course the influx of European ideas could
not be arrested. Whereas before both Church and State had remained dominant and stable in conservative Spain, the ideas of
Darwinism and modern science began to upset this stability.
The unsettling ideas of Schopenhauer with his pessimistic emphasis on the will, the revolutionary ideas of Nietzsche, the existential anguish of Kierkegaard—the thinking of these and many
others became live issues in Spain to be either defended or attacked. Various other "schools" in the literary area—Symbolism, Impressionism, Decadentism—generally indicated a modern
direction toward more emphasis upon the individual, toward
fragmentation of a cultural conformity which had previously

existed. The founding of the Free Institute (*La Institución Libre de Enseñanza*) in 1876, rigidly separated from Church and State and dedicated to free inquiry into all the problems of mankind, became an important liberal force in propagating the European ideas in Spanish culture.

Toward the end of the century, the new generation (which became the so-called Generation of 98) was in rebellion against the ideals of the previous one, and in the novel, the drama, and in poetry, the older writers fell into disfavor. The novels of Alarcón, Valera, and Palacio Valdés became period pieces. The regional novelist Pereda, usually a spokesman for localism and traditionalism, passed out of favor. Only the great novelist Galdós, himself a liberal, managed to bridge the gap between the generations. In the drama, José Echegaray, given to exaggerated plot and bombastic dialogue, became a special target of the new generation, in spite of the fact that he ultimately received the Nobel Prize for Literature.

In poetry, which is our special concern with Antonio Machado, the state of decline was acute toward the end of the century. Gustavo Bécquer had died prematurely in 1870, Rosalía de Castro in 1885. In the 1890's the Romantic poet Zorrilla was still living, but his poetry was forgotten. Ramón de Campoamor was considered great in his day, but by now his philosophical and ironic commentaries were felt to be commonplace and trite. Núñez de Arce still represented the grandiloquent manner and the public voice; both were rapidly losing favor. When in this period the renovation in poetry began, it is significant that the new direction began in Spanish America with Rubén Darío, an indication of Spanish decline and of the cultural maturity of the young Hispanic nations.

By the end of the 19th century, two important literary groups were developing strongly and rapidly among the new generation. The first, associated with the Generation of 98, was led initially by Miguel de Unamuno and Angel Ganivet, and concerned itself with the destiny of Spain, with the problem of the country's past and future. In the first group, as early as 1895 Unamuno published a series of dense articles attempting to explore and analyze the eternal Spanish values. In 1897 Ganivet published his *Idearium español*, a book-length essay treating of the causes of Spain's decline and offering a general program for recovery. The group pursued the difficult task of renovating Spain without losing her traditional values, without excessive Europeanization. The other group, which generally espoused what is called Modernism in the Hispanic countries and which was led by Rubén Darío, constituted more specifically a literary movement concerned with renovation of forms, increased subjectivity, and personal artistic creation, characteristics of the French schools of Symbolism and Impressionism. The two groups were at first directly in opposition, but gradually they tended to merge in the authors of the Generation of 98, each individual developing the particular concerns of his own personality. Antonio Machado, as one of the younger members of the Generation, began his poetic career after both these currents were established in Spanish literature.

II   *A Patio in Seville*

Antonio Machado came from a family of both influence and talent in Andalusia. His paternal grandfather, Antonio Machado Núñez, for whom the poet was named, enjoyed a varied and illustrious career, in both the intellectual and the political fields. After failing to win fortune in the New World, he went to Paris and completed his medical studies. He returned to Seville to practice medicine, but soon became disenchanted, apparently, with the limitations and narrowness of the medical field. However, he retained an interest in the sciences in general, and founded and edited an influential journal of philosophy and science in Seville. In politics he must have been successful also, for in 1870 he was governor of the province of Seville.

His son and our poet's father, Antonio Machado Alvarez (in Spanish the final family name is the mother's) continued the strong intellectual achievement. After receiving his degree in Letters (or liberal arts), he attended law school at the University of Seville and earned his law degree, although he never practiced the profession. His primary interest became the folklore of Spain, especially the Andalusian flamenco song and poetry. He became an authority in this field, ultimately publishing at least four important collections. Years later our poet evoked a powerful childhood memory of his father—"high forehead / imperial beard and drooping mustache"—as he read, meditated over, and even hummed his beloved flamenco songs in his study.

The poet's mother was Doña Ana Ruiz Hernández, who became a typical Spanish wife and mother, constantly making her own needs the needs of her family. A small person with dark eyes and complexion as is usual in Andalusia, Doña Ana's outstanding characteristic was her vivacity and sparkle in conversation. Joaquín Malo de Molina, who much later was a student of Antonio's, recalls how he used to enjoy talking with Doña Ana when he visited in the Machado home.[2] She had no intellectual pretensions, but was a refuge for her son throughout his life.

As an indication of their socially prominent position, in the early 1870's the Machados were living in the Palacio de las Dueñas, an ancient family home of the Dukes of Alba, located within the city of Seville. Their first-born son, who arrived in 1874, was named Manuel. Destined himself to become an important poet of the aesthetic *modernista* movement, Manuel was to remain close in spirit to his brother Antonio. Antonio was born on July 26, 1875. Later two more brothers were born; José, who was to become a painter, and Joaquín.

Antonio spent his early childhood years in the impressive setting of the Palace. Its privacy assured by surrounding walls, the palace has an expansive patio of three divisions. In one a fountain murmurs; in another the dark lemon trees grow; in all the brilliant flowers typical of Andalusia bloom in varied colors. The brilliant sunlight of Seville emphasizes the contrasts between white walls and dark trees. Later Machado was to elaborate poetic symbols from impressions received here, especially the fountain, in "a bright garden where the lemon tree ripens its fruit." Blended with these personal impressions were his first experiences with the world of reading. Apparently his grandmother often assembled the children for listening to the ballads of Spanish history, the "Legends" of the poet Bécquer, and even selections from Shakespeare and Dickens in translation.

The poet later "recreated" some of his strongest childhood impressions as he became obsessed with time and memory. He liked to recall the time, actually during the courtship of his

parents, when a school of dolphins lost its way and came from
the sea up the Guadalquivir River all the way to Seville. Apparently his mother must have told and retold the details of this
event, for it became almost a "real" experience in the poet's
memory.[3] In his gentle, ironic manner, Machado also fancifully
traced much of his philosophical insight back to an early experience with his mother. As the two were out walking, the boy
Antonio was enjoying a stalk of sugarcane, when he saw another
boy who also had a stalk. Antonio was sure his was bigger, but
when he asked his mother for corroboration of his opinion she
replied sharply, "No, son, where are your eyes?"[4] Thus Machado
traced to this moment his preoccupation with the problem of
getting beyond the self to a proper awareness of otherness before perceptions can be valid. The eight years Antonio lived in
the Palace in Seville were years of tranquility and stability.

III   *Youth in Madrid*

In 1883 Antonio's grandfather was appointed to a professor-
ship in the Central University in Madrid, and the whole family
moved there. They took a house of ample size on Claudio Coella
Street, but as is typical of Madrid, it was actually an apartment
of an entire floor in a multistoried building. For the family, life
in Madrid in the following years proved to be turbulent in comparison with the peaceful time spent in the Palace in Seville. A
close friend of the family was arrested for political reasons and
barely escaped with his life. In 1885 an epidemic of cholera
scourged the city, but the family escaped without harm. The
family changed houses a surprising number of times, generally
moving into more modest dwellings.

Since the family was already given to the liberal-scientific
tradition, the three older boys were enrolled in the Free Institute in 1883, a significant step for their future development.[5]
Since almost all the schools were traditionally run by religious
orders, the Free Institute had been founded in 1876 by Francisco Giner (whose family was close to the Machados) and
others as a school dedicated to free inquiry into all the problems of mankind. The school was specifically separated from
the influences of both Church and State. The philosophy which

reigned in the Free Institute was generally called *Krausismo*, [6] after an obscure German philosopher named Krause but developed in Spain by Julián Sanz del Río and others. The group of liberals who became followers of Krausism fought to develop a new educational system in Spain. Although the Free Institute dedicated itself to developing students of high ethical principles, social responsibility, and brotherhood, the school was unyielding in its negative attitude toward the Catholic Church as an institution. Although Antonio was only a boy during the years he studied in the Free Institute, he continued to support and develop the ideas of the school throughout his life. Actually he finished his secondary schooling in the religious Institutes of San Isidro and of Cardinal Cisneros in Madrid. Then his formal education lapsed until ten years later when he resumed work on a degree in *Filosofía y Letras* (Liberal Arts).

About the time Antonio finished this schooling, the Machado family began to suffer declining fortune, and then tragedy struck. During this period Antonio's father was apparently content with publishing the results of his study of Andalusian folklore and flamenco song, but apparently his scholarship produced little income for his family. The continuing changes of residence seem to indicate a financial problem. Finally Antonio's father (apparently in 1892) decided to improve his situation by going to Puerto Rico as a recorder of property titles. Early the next year, however, he became dangerously ill, and he was brought back only as far as Seville, where he died in 1893, without getting to see his family again. The grandfather, Antonio Machado Núñez, died in 1895, leaving the family in very precarious circumstances. It is surprising that Machado was very slow in assuming family responsibilities, for he continued to live a somewhat Bohemian life, writing broad satire, flirting with a career in the theater, journeying to France—with no observable direction toward a profession.

After 1892, the young Antonio was striking out in directions which do not seem to fit the later stereotype of his personality, but continued study of his life and work have of course revealed the inadequacy of the stereotype. Machado's initial production as a writer was a series of short satirical sketches. In 1892 he and Manuel became acquainted with Enrique Paradas, editor of a new journal, *La Caricatura*, whom Antonio was to remember even forty years later as a master of the *copla*, a short popular stanza, which often contains a distilled comment on life. Antonio wrote under the pseudonym *Cabellera* (by which he apparently meant "Longhair"), his brother Manuel was *Polilla*, the "Moth"; the brothers also collaborated on a series of sketches of political satire in *La Caricatura.*

The eleven sketches of Antonio which survive[7] are interesting examples of broad satire, humorous but never vicious. The types satirized are the would-be artists (poets, actors, bullfighters) striving without the necessary talent to crash the artistic world in Madrid—as Antonio himself was dreaming of doing. There is the would-be heroic poet, reading the interminable stanzas of his neo-epic to a captive audience in the *tertulia*, the traditional literary gathering. There is the bullfight fan (not a fighter, only a fan), who is attempting through his utter dedication to turn his fandom into a profession. There is also a peek into the life of the sub-theaters in Madrid. In style, young Antonio sustains a high level of vocabulary and rounded periods (with an occasional Homeric simile); and with this style he elaborates his scruffy materials, occasionally descending to the slang of the day. Even at this stage he shows signs of the talent for writing prose he was to develop throughout his career.

In addition to his budding literary interests, during the 1890's Antonio became fascinated with the world of the theater, not as a dramatist but as an actor. At this time one of the Machados' intimate friends was Ricardo Calvo, born into a family of actors and destined himself to become a star of the first magnitude. Another friend was Antonio de Zayas, later the Duke of Amalfi, who was also strongly attracted to the theater. Although the dapper Manuel seemed more the actor type, Antonio himself as a young man was tall, attractive, and possessed a fine speaking voice. He finally persuaded a friend to secure for him a position in the theatrical company of Fernando Díaz de Mendoza. After a miserable apprenticeship he was finally given a nine-word speaking part as an Assyrian soldier in a drama of Calderón. Thus ended his acting career; immediately thereafter he confined himself to attacking the neo-Romantic exaggerations of José Echegaray, then Madrid's most popular dramatist.

Toward the end of the century, the family still being in a difficult financial situation, both Antonio and Manuel fortunately found a way of combining their growing literary interests with a paying position. In 1899 first Manuel, then Antonio, went to Paris as translators in the publishing house of the Garnier brothers, then developing a series of Spanish editions. Exactly what the Machados did has remained unclear, since no books bearing their names have been discovered. At least they were plunged into the exciting literary atmosphere of Paris. Later, from his many impressions, Antonio preferred to remember that Symbolism in poetry and Impressionism in painting were reigning movements. He also recalled meeting Oscar Wilde, by then a broken figure, and Jean Moreas, a poet of Greek origin important in the Symbolist movement. At the time there was a colony of Spaniards and Latin-American literary figures in the French capital, among them the Guatemalan Gómez Carrillo. Antonio stayed only four months before returning to Madrid. He was still unsettled, still without a profession. But through Gómez Carrillo he secured the unlikely post of Vice-Consul of Guatemala in Paris and returned there. This time he met the great Nicaraguan poet Rubén Darío, who became an important though brief inspirer of his poetry. After another short stay Antonio left Paris. Although French literature was not to be a decisive influence on his work, and in fact he often attacked many elements of French culture, he nevertheless became a professor of French and spent his mature life teaching it.

At the same time that he was exploring these interests, Antonio Machado was also reading, discussing, and beginning to write poetry, which of course was to bring him lasting fame. Since Machado preferred not to discuss the years of his poetic formation, not many specific details are available. We know that he read the melancholy Galician poetess Rosalía de Castro and also Gustavo Bécquer, a Sevillian like Machado. He studied avidly an anthology of the poems of Paul Verlaine, and near the end of the century he discovered Rubén Darío. Machado indicated that he started writing as early as 1899, but his first surviving poems were not published until 1901, in *Electra*. The poet Juan Ramón Jiménez later cleared up what seemed to be a small mystery: Jiménez, who was annoyed that two of his earliest books survived, insisted that Antonio had really written a collection of *Cantares* (*Songs*), but later had destroyed all the copies.

During the time Antonio and Manuel were in France, both were working seriously on books of poetry. Manuel's, entitled *Alma* (*Soul*), was published in 1901. The success of *Soul* must have spurred Antonio's efforts, for in late 1902 his small volume *Soledades* (*Solitudes*) appeared; it was, however, dated as of 1903. At the time of the book's appearance, Antonio was in Granada and Córdoba, where Ricardo Calvo was staging a play by Ramón del Valle-Inclán. When Machado returned to Madrid, his book was enjoying a measure of success.

Almost immediately, however, Antonio was experiencing dissatisfaction with the little book. Certain of the poems in it were aesthetic, plastic, or Parnassian (characteristics of the *modernista* movement then in vogue in Spain); certain others revealed what Machado was later to call a "palpitation of spirit." Little by little he began to disown the aesthetic poems and to write further poems with more emphasis on the spiritual and the ethical. During the next four years he organized, collected, and wrote the poems for a greatly expanded *Solitudes*, from which he actually suppressed a number of the earlier poems.

During this period of spiritual growth and of rapid maturing as a poet, the influence of Miguel de Unamuno on Antonio Machado is of decisive importance.[8] In the early 1890's Unamuno had gained prominence with a series of essays through a study of Spain's history, language, and customs. In an epoch in which the artists were often retreating from life into art, Unamuno in a serious and usually strident voice was crying out for a deepening of spirit: life as a spiritual battle is our constant image of him. Machado sent Unamuno a copy of the 1903 *Solitudes*, which in general was favorably received. In 1904 Unamuno published a long open letter to Machado in the journal *Helios*.[9] In the letter he urges Machado directly to forsake completely the doctrine of "art for art's sake," the undue emphasis on the aesthetic, which the Spanish tend to associate with the French. "The profession of poet is one of the most odious I know," declares Unamuno; that is, one must be a man, a man of spirit. By 1905, in an article on Unamuno's personal re-creation of Cervantes' Don Quijote, *Life of Don Quijote and*

Sancho, Machado indicates his fervent admiration for Unamuno. "What I consciously admire in Unamuno is his heroic and constant spiritual activity." He goes on to say that the book "is impregnated with such profound and potent feeling, that the ideas of the thinker acquire the force and expression of a poet's images. . . . Only feeling is creative."[10]

As a practical result of his contact with Unamuno, Machado turned away from his semi-Bohemian habits of a decade and began seriously to prepare himself for a profession. During the year 1906 Antonio retired regularly to his rooms to devote himself to the study of Spanish and French grammar and literature, with the purpose of preparing himself as a professor in the Institutes (secondary schools), many of them in the provinces. Rather than attend the university, he chose to study privately and then to face the dreaded *oposiciones*, where the judges over long periods test the candidates, often having them compete face to face. Fortunately a young professor[11] who suffered with (and against) Machado has later described how in early 1907 those "oppositions" dragged on for three months. He recalls how both he and Antonio, faced with translating a well-known sonnet of Verlaine, translated it into sonnet form in Spanish. Obviously the examinations were indeed thorough and technically difficult. Both candidates won positions; Antonio chose the Institute in Baeza, but for some unexplained reason he actually went to Soria. Thus ended an epoch in cosmopolitan living; hereafter he was to know the solitude of the provincial towns.

IV   *Five Years in Soria*

In the summer of 1907 Antonio Machado went up to Soria officially to take charge of his position, came back to Madrid to settle his affairs, then returned in October to begin his teaching duties.[12] Soria, lying in the Castilian highlands about 140 miles northeast of Madrid, enjoys a beautiful natural location, the details of which Machado was to immortalize through Spanish poetry. The Duero river flows "like a crossbow's arc" around the town, itself in a bowl surrounded by hills. Off to the East lies Moncayo mountain and the historic land of Aragón; off to the West rises an imposing bluff called the Frente, which Machado strangely never mentioned. Upriver a few miles are the ruins of Numancia, a Roman fortress town whose history was immortalized by Cervantes in a drama. Soria itself was an important city in the Middle Ages, but in 1907 it had declined into a quiet provincial town, although during Machado's years there four journals were being published. Soria is typical of Castilian towns in that it can boast two cathedrals, one of them Romanesque, the private palace of the Gomara family, at present vacant and in shabby condition, and on a hill overlooking the town, a medieval castle almost completely in ruins.

Always unassuming and patient, Machado apparently adjusted without too much agony to the routine of teaching in the atmosphere of the Institute. His modest poetic fame and his experience in Paris became known, but he did not attempt to exploit either. In the Institute, run heavy-handedly by an aging director, there were two sharply divided political groups. Machado ignored local politics in his kindly way, without snubbing its practitioners. Little by little he became acquainted with a few men with strong cultural interests, for example Manuel Ayuso and José María Palacio, whose names appear in his literary work. His teaching apparently drifted into the normal Spanish pattern. In spite of the *Krausista* insistence on a new teacher-student relationship, Machado in practice could not bridge the gulf. Even in the secondary school students learned by rote memory and by endless repetition. Formalized sets of things—countries and capitals, Spanish verb forms, lines of Kings —were memorized and repeated, with little real thinking involved. In the classroom itself, it seems that Machado from the beginning expected little and demanded almost nothing of his students, and his lessons were taught without enthusiasm.

Of Soria, Machado was to say later with utmost simplicity, "There I was married; there died my wife, whose memory accompanies me always." Despite his normally attractive appearance, Machado as a young man was timid and unaggressive, and until he was beyond thirty romantic episodes are missing from his life. Of course his whole Generation of 1898 was, in general, unromantic, placing the blame on Spanish social customs. It was apparently in late 1907 that Antonio met Leonor Izquierdo, daughter of a Civil Guard and the lady in whose boardinghouse he stayed. Leonor at the time was a lass of only thirteen, so that Antonio had to wait a whole year before beginning to court her officially.

They were married in July, 1909, in the ancient Romanesque church of Santa María la Mayor. Antonio was then nearly thirty-five, the bride only sixteen. A surviving wedding picture reveals Leonor to be small, with dark eyes and hair and fair skin; the groom was stiff and somewhat elegant in black. On the honeymoon, as provincials with limited resources still do, they visited the nearby towns of Zaragoza and Pamplona. Then the couple returned to Madrid to stay with his family for a time, so that Leonor could go to the theater and enjoy the attractions of the city. Leonor was a simple, provincial girl of limited education, but apparently Antonio was content with his new life.

After another year of teaching, in 1911 Machado secured a fellowship and obtained leave from his teaching position to study in Paris. At this time, he finished the manuscript of his new book of poetry and sent it to the editor Martínez Sierra. *Campos de Castilla (Fields of Castile)* reflects his new objective outlook through his intimate contact with Soria. It also develops the broader theme of Spain through a preoccupation with her past and future (to be discussed later). Leonor was thrilled and Antonio no doubt pleased to be going to France under different circumstances. In Paris Machado followed with interest some lectures of Bédier, but he apparently attended a whole course taught by the philosopher Henri Bergson, then enjoying outstanding popularity. Bergson's emphasis on the importance of intuition and the definition of time struck a responsive chord in Machado, whose earlier poetry is related to these areas. The poet was also still in a creative period; at the time he was working on a long poem, *La tierra de Alvargonzález (The Land of Alvargonzález)*, which he hoped would be a capital addition to the volume *Fields of Castile.*

At this time, his good fortune as a man at its zenith, impending tragedy struck. Leonor, who apparently inherited a disposition toward illness, suddenly began hemorrhaging, one of the signs of advanced tuberculosis. Antonio, who had not borne serious responsibilities before, suffered a harrowing experience in finding a doctor for her, since the attack occurred on an important French holiday. After she stayed a month in the hospital in Paris, he brought her back to Soria, and it became obvious that she would not recover. The following months were excruciating for Antonio. He rented for them a small house with a garden on the hill near the old Mirón monastery; he made a kind of cart for her so that he could keep her outside in the sunlight. But on August 1, 1912, she died, and the Church buried her in the Espino Cemetery. Antonio could no longer bear the memories of Soria, and soon he asked for and received a transfer to the Institute in Baeza, in the South of Spain.

V   *Solitude in Baeza*

It was late in 1912 that Antonio Machado fled from Soria, as usual riding the train with its third-class coaches which have the closely-spaced wooden seats. He reached Baeza in a seriously depressed condition, so that the town of course failed to impress him. Baeza lies on the Guadalquivir River in the province of Jaén, between the Manchegan country of Castile and Andalusia.[13] The town has a fine plaza with a Town Hall in the Renaissance style. The Institute in which Machado was destined to teach once housed a great university.

During the first year in Baeza, Machado remained in a dangerously depressed condition. His mother went down from Madrid and lived with him for a time. Soon after Leonor's death, the poet, not given to histrionics, wrote to his friend Juan Ramón Jiménez: "When I lost my wife, I thought about shooting myself." He continues, in words reflecting the influence of the ethical teaching of the Free Institute: "The success of my book [*Fields of Castile*] saved me, and not because of vanity . . . but because I thought that if there was in me a useful power I didn't have the right to destroy it."[14] Even a year or more later he confessed to Unamuno that he had not recovered; his problem was intensified because Leonor's death shook his faith in life itself, she being "an angelical creature cut down cruelly by death."[15]

He turned for consolation to philosophy, and at least he gradually recovered the will to go on with his work. While in Baeza he began a systematic study of philosophy, at least partly with the idea of earning a liberal arts degree in the University. Undoubtedly stimulated by Unamuno's example, he tried to learn to read Greek, so as to be able to understand Plato and Aristotle in the original. Given his late start, the task proved too much for him. He also had to develop some competence in Latin as a requirement for the degree. There survives a letter to the professor who was to test him on the subject, more or less pleading for mercy because of his lateness in starting his study. His later prose writings indicate that he studied Descartes, Kant, Hegel, and Leibnitz. His whole generation read, or at least read those who had read, Nietzsche and Schopenhauer. He surely mastered Bergson's important book, *Time and Free Will.* A few years later he was to reveal that, while his reading of literature had always been desultory, he had read in philosophy with some order.

In Baeza Machado continued the habits of Soria in spending the summers in Madrid, but now each summer he was taking examinations in the University of Madrid. Finally, in 1918, he went up for a final oral examination, undoubtedly a frightful prospect for a student of forty-three. The examiners themselves were formidable. One of them was José Ortega y Gasset, then a young professor whose brilliance as a thinker, writer, and scholar was fast becoming evident. Thereafter Machado was qualified to use the coveted title of doctor, but he never did.

In Baeza Machado gradually returned to his ancient habits of life. His afternoon walks were perhaps a therapy for his inner strife and unrest. A student of his, Joaquín Malo de Molina, remembers how his professor of French would sometimes walk all the way to Ubeda, more than five miles, "for a cup of coffee," he explained with sardonic humor. By this time he was walking with the slow purposeless gait everyone recalls; Malo explains that actually Machado was slightly lame in his right foot. Also in this period he assumed the personal appearance everyone remembers. He became heavier, and his disregard for his dress almost reached being a distinction. His shapeless hat, baggy, worn-out suit covered with ashes, the ancient tie carelessly knotted— such was his image among the Generation of 1898.

Machado also found another *tertulia*, a gathering with a fixed cast of members, in Baeza. In the Institute he became acquainted with Adolfo Almazán, a professor of Physical Education in the Institute, who also doubled as the town druggist. In his pharmacy, the pride of which was a great, heartwarming stove, a compatible group including Machado spent many evening hours in conversation or in meditation. Another regular member was Cristóbal Torres, a local lawyer with few cases and much leisure time. Torres, an intelligent, thoughtful man, was an indefatigable walker like Machado, so that the two proved to be very compatible. The three friends even organized an excursion to visit the source of the Guadalquivir River in the mountains near Cazorla. For Machado, this was to repeat an excursion he had made to the source of the Duero in the mountains toward Aragón.

In his isolated post in Baeza, Machado nevertheless occasionally participated in the literary homages which have been a part of Spanish culture. Because of his great respect for Azorín, who was writing books of poetic prose on Castile, one summer Machado, with Ortega, Cossío, and others, went to Aranjuez to a program to honor Azorín for his *Castile*. There in the setting of the royal gardens of the old palace in Aranjuez, Machado participated directly by reading his "From My Corner," a poem praising Azorín and exalting Castile at the same time.

In 1915 a first meeting took place between the two poets who have become the greats of their century. There arrived from Granada a group led by Professor Martín Domínguez, an old friend of Machado's, for a cultural gathering in Baeza. Among the group was Federico García Lorca, then only a youth. Machado read from his poem *The Land of Alvargonzález*; Lorca played on the piano some compositions of Manuel de Falla and some Spanish folk songs. Much later, Machado was to write a gripping poem after Lorca was shot during the Civil War.

Gradually in Baeza, as Machado began to recover from the shock of his wife's death, he continued to develop his ideas as a critic of Spanish society. His personal correspondence[16] with Unamuno reveals that he was thinking, and thinking seriously, about Spanish problems. His analysis of Baeza as exemplary of Spain (excluding Madrid) is merciless and pessimistic. Baeza, he

declares, boasts of an Institute, a Seminary, a School of Arts,
and several secondary schools, but hardly thirty percent of the
people can read. The only bookstore sells mainly postcards, de-
votional materials, and pornography. And, of great importance,
the young men of the educated class are ruined by their frivoli-
ties, especially gambling of various types. There is overwhelming
piety, or lip service to religion, says Machado, but no real religion. Machado, like Ganivet and Unamuno before him, is calling
for a return to the development of serious and virtuous men, in
the ancient sense of the words. What religion there is in Baeza is
dominated by the women, a tendency Machado deplores. In his
discussions with Unamuno, Machado's thought is developing toward a restatement of the principle of Christian charity, as Jesus
himself expressed it. Earlier both men had written on the Cain-
Abel theme as it applied to Spain; it is surprising at this point to
find Machado advising Unamuno to turn from the Old Testa-
ment theme of envy and to write a "Christian novel." At this
time Machado was not ready to become an activist; he did not
even dare to say these "certain things in public." But he is obviously preparing himself to do so, and he recognizes that his
years in the isolation of the small town have been fruitful
ones for his thought.

Throughout the years in Baeza Antonio Machado continued
his poetic production, although at times the springs of his inspiration almost ran dry. He wrote to his friend Xavier Valcarce
that he could no longer sing, confessing that the enigma of life
and the abrupt tragedy of losing his wife had driven him to
philosophical speculation. However, he completed the cycle of
poetry begun in Soria. Now the landscape of Soria becomes one
purified in his memory and remembrance. His poems of love explore the effects of her presence in his memory and lament the
great damage of her loss. Moreover, he finished the cycle of
poems in praise of worthy contemporaries. The deaths of Francisco Giner and Rubén Darío evoked meaningful tributes, and
the living examples of Azorín, Unamuno, Valle-Inclán and
Ortega y Gasset provided him specific themes. Machado endeav-
ored to make his poems of praise honest tributes and meaningful
lyrics at the same time, and it is significant that when, for example, his youthful enthusiasm for Valle-Inclán became qualified
approval, he honestly changed a dedication to this figure.

In Baeza Machado continued to develop the philosophical-stoic manner he had begun in a section of "Proverbs and Songs" in *Fields of Castile*. As the title of the section suggests, these poems were often a single quotation of short lines, containing an essential drop of hard-gained wisdom and satire, in the manner of proverbs; and they were cast in the form of the Andalusian popular *copla*, long one of his interests. Machado also attempted to respond to the Baezan landscape as he had to that around Soria, but he simply no longer could, in any whole-hearted sense. In one major poem, he attempted to make a symbol out of the Andalusian olive tree, in comparison with the Castilian oak, but even here the long poem has a classical background, with Demeter and other Greek figures of mythology. In spite of his limited production, his growing reputation was responsible for two books of poetry being published. In 1917, the publishing house Calleja printed a *Poesía escogida* (*Selected Poems*), and the Residence of Students in Madrid (which grew out of the Free Institute) published *Poesías completas* (*Complete Poems*). These books served to consolidate his reputation as the poet of his generation, his main competition being Juan Ramón Jiménez. It was 1924 before Machado published some of the Baeza poems, a book of *Nuevas canciones* (*New Songs*), and the unspecific title indicates the weakening of his poetic inspiration.

At heart Machado never quite settled down in Baeza. As early as 1914 he told Unamuno in a letter that he was "resigned, but not satisfied" there, but that he preferred not to go through the official process of intriguing and begging in order to be transferred. Again in 1915, it seemed that Unamuno was going to help him secure a position in Salamanca, but this never materialized. Machado even contemplated entering the competition for a place in the Institute in Alicante, in order to use it as a stepping-stone for another transfer. Finally in 1919 he succeeded in gaining a vacant position in Segovia, and the poet headed north toward Castile.

VI   *Segovia and Madrid*

Antonio Machado was fortunate that the vicissitudes of his existence found him in some of the most strikingly located of the Spanish towns, towns rich in historical tradition. Segovia, then and now a small town less than fifty miles northwest of Madrid, has a stunning location and monuments which are a constant outstanding visual reminder of history. Running from the nearby hills and into the heart of town is the great, double-tiered aqueduct, a marvel of ancient Roman engineering. On the other side of town, at the confluence of the small rivers Eresma and Clamores, the Alcázar, or castle, truly towers over the landscape, a reminder of Segovia's strategic position in the Middle Ages. Moreover, a great cathedral rises in the center of town. During the long period from 1919 to 1931, Machado was to live in Segovia, but for him there was only one Soria—he could not respond to the Castilian spirit in the living history of Segovia. In his first years he continued to deepen his philosophical, political, and even educational ideas, and to express them in prose form; and he made an attempt to put into practice some of his educational ideas. Little by little, however, he began to spend his weekdays of toil in Segovia, but on weekends he escaped to Madrid, where he pursued his real interests, especially in the theater. His poetic production from these years, while very sparse, is of a varied nature and an extremely high quality. Above all, after his years of solitude in Baeza, Machado seemed disposed to enter the world again.

Soon he reestablished his outward habits of many years. Again he took lodgings in a boardinghouse on Desamparados Street, a cramped room with a little stove, a narrow metal bed. As usual, it was soon overrunning with books. From his home he made his way to the Institute; by now everyone greeted him as "Don Antonio," though he was only about 45. His bedraggled appearance became even more pronounced, his walk more shuffling.

In the early 1920's, Segovia was for Machado and a select group of friends "a small Renaissance court."[17] Their meeting place was in the potter Fernando Arranz' shop, which was a converted Romanesque church. The people who met there after school and work hours were men of ideas. Don Antonio was the most famous member of the group, but he bore with patience and resignation the discussions of more mediocre members. Don Blas Zembrano, a professor in the Normal School, was a regular;

the sculptor Emiliano Barral, who later did a bust of Machado, and his father were also usually present. The oldest member of the group was Father Villalba, a former Augustinian priest. There were also three men of letters whose star was rising: Julián Otero, Mariano Quintanilla, and Ignacio Corral. The group often developed their discussions from reading Ortega y Gasset's outstanding scholarly journal, *La Revista de Occidente*, and the most prominent of the French journals then being published.

When the weather was not too bad, the group always walked through Segovia. The route was not usually varied; they trudged by a certain ancient Mudéjar church, went under the Aqueduct, reached the highway leading out of town and then returned. The excursion would be quite long and strenuous, because of the hilly terrain around Segovia. In both the *tertulia* and the walks, Don Antonio largely kept both his personal anguish and his joy to himself, apparently revealing only a few political ideas. His friends were not really aware of the ideas and projects teeming in his mind.

Soon after his arrival in Segovia, Machado learned that an activist group was trying to found a Popular University, with free public lectures and a lending library. Apparently he eagerly supported the project. Activities were first conducted in the Normal School; later the school held its meetings in a reconditioned church. Machado had brought to Segovia his developing philosophy of an active Christian brotherhood, outside the hierarchy of the Catholic Church. This philosophy soon developed political overtones. In 1920 he published a brief article called "By Mistake," in which he satirizes the present system of "justice" being practiced in Spain, specifically attacking the oppression on the part of the Civil Guard. In fact, says Machado ironically in one of his gnomic poems, what the ruling class wants for the poor is not justice, but "justices," to protect the rich man's house. As a further indication of his expanded activities, Machado himself delivered a lecture "On Russian Literature"[18] for the program of the Popular University. The lecture shows evidences of his usual intelligent penetration. Although Machado declares the Russian Revolution already a failure because Russia lacks sufficient philosophical tradition, he finds a universality in

Russian literature because it projects an idea of Christian, human brotherhood. For Machado, Tolstoy was "the synthesis of the Russian spirit"; and indeed, the Spaniard's Christian philosophy was basically Tolstoyan, although developed also from other sources. The Popular University prospered for a few years, but apparently the dream died without becoming a permanent educational force in Segovia.

When we piece together years later all the available details of Antonio Machado's life, it becomes obvious that around 1926 he suffered (or enjoyed) what can only be called a crisis, as Justina Ruiz de Conde has indicated.[19] The crisis had years of incubation. Machado in Segovia was becoming discontented with both his own personality and his literary image as a poet in isolation with a few fading memories. Moreover, he of course had his pride, and the poets of his generation were being jostled by the new generation, that of García Lorca. In one of his proverbs, he indicated that he disliked the Italian dictum *O rinnovarsi o perire*, but of course he had to live with it. In 1924, Machado rediscovered his old interest in the theater, now as author rather than actor, and he joined his brother Manuel first in modernizing some Golden Age Spanish plays for presentation. In 1924 he published his *New Songs* (which were not very new), almost his last book under his own name. Hereafter he was to write behind a *persona*, such as Abel Martín (note the initials) and Juan de Mairena.

Machado was also experiencing a rejuvenation of his emotional life. In 1921 love for him was still "distance and horizon: absence," but he soon begins a dialogue with an imaginary lady, and there is a repeated image of blooming spring. This rebirth of the desire for love finally became a reality—at least his love was a reality; he confessed it clearly in a sonnet: "*Nel mezzo del camin*, the arrow of an untimely love pierced my heart." Machado called her Guiomar in his later poetry, and for a long time everyone (even his biographer Pérez Ferrero) assumed she was a figment of his imagination. Therefore it came as a stunning surprise in 1950 when the novelist Concha Espina, in a book romanticized to the point of silliness, published a series of love letters (along with reproductions of the originals) which Antonio wrote to Guiomar. As love letters (and not as literary exercises), they are grippingly authentic, with that ring of sincerity and truth so characteristic of Machado. Since Espina left Guiomar's real name shrouded in mystery, there has been a rush to discover her identity.

And working backwards, it is not too difficult. In a letter of early 1929 to Unamuno, Machado slips in this line: "A few days ago I sent to you with our *Juan de Mañara* [a drama of his and Manuel's] the book *Huerto cerrado (Closed Garden)* of Pilar Valderrama. This lady, whom I met in Segovia . . ." Now Antonio, like a schoolboy bursting with his secret, is momentarily blinded to the fact that Unamuno was a most unlikely choice to share such an exchange. Unamuno's great disappointment was that he never had enjoyed a profound romantic love; moreover, he was sure that women preferred (and probably were only capable of) a state of domesticity. Later, in 1930, Machado published an article giving strong praise to Pilar's poetry, even though it was much out of fashion at the moment. Actually the two met at least as early as 1926. Malo de Molina remembers clearly (since he was stunned to see Don Antonio alone with a lady) that he saw them at a performance of Benavente's *The Passion Flower* in Madrid in the spring of 1926.

The essential biographical details on Pilar de Valderrama have been provided by Justina Ruiz de Conde.[20] Born in Madrid in 1899 (and thus a quarter-century younger than Antonio), she received the normal training of girls of her social class, her family being well-to-do landowners. Shy and sensitive, Pilar was married at twenty to a young engineer who later developed theatrical interests. In the early 1920's the couple started a family of three children. Apparently Pilar gradually created a kind of salon in her home, with special emphasis on drama. Interestingly, a member of the group was Concha Espina. In a poem in *Closed Garden*, Pilar hints that "there are few souls, very few,/ which have not their tragedy." For Antonio, this autumn love was foredoomed to anguish, given the strong ethical bent of his nature. However, for years he carried on a passionate correspondence with her, often saw her alone in their "corner" of a little café in Madrid, took at least one long trip to see her during her vacations in San Sebastián and once bought her an expensive present.

Pilar de Valderrama thus accepted his devotion, but returned little of it. Of course she must have considered herself the unattainable ideal, a living symbol of inspiration for him. Despite Machado's public praise of her poetry, it is generally mediocre. Machado picked out of it a few brief lyrics in his own Andalusian *copla* manner which are striking; the rest wavers between piety and smugness—this latter quality because of a too-easy triumph of the "spiritual" over the lowly senses. However, in spite of the provocative title of *Closed Garden*, her poetry during these years is almost silent on their companionship and above all lacks passion, in marked contrast to Antonio's during this period. Like a medieval lady, she received the homage of her aging knight; later Machado was to say, with irony but not without truth, that he developed his metaphysical system from this experience.

After 1925, although Machado continued to labor during the week as a professor in Segovia, every weekend he took the train to Madrid where his interests were. The route across the Guadarrama Mountains and the first view of distant Madrid is a striking one. On one of the countless times he made the journey, he wrote a poem which captures the scenes, concentrating especially on a sanatorium high in the mountains and the human experiences he imagines must be transpiring there. In Madrid he and his brother Manuel worked on their plays; their first effort, *Julianillo Valcárcel*, a drama of the Golden Age, was premiered in 1926. Encouraged by a modest success, the Machados thereafter for a number of years sought to enhance their reputation with a new play each theatrical season. Their outstanding triumph was to be *La Lola* (*La Lola se va a los puertos*) of 1929, in which the influence of Guiomar on Antonio is clearly evident.

Except for the drama, Antonio Machado's important original work after 1925 was confined to two books, both open-ended and sometimes not quite distinct from the other. In 1926 he published *De un cancionero apócrifo* (*From an Apocryphal Songbook*), in which his first important *persona* Abel Martín appears. The brief but intensely concentrated book is an expression of Machado's persistent conviction that the poet always wavers between philosophy and poetry, poetry and philosophy. Abel Martín insists that all great poets must have a metaphysics, implied but of course not expressed in poetry. In fact, Abel foresaw the day (and Machado undoubtedly trusted it had arrived in him) when the poet and philosopher would be one. (He suspected that thus far only Plato could exemplify this position.) In the prose parts of the book, Machado presents his elaboration of his basic philosophical ideas: the "essential heterogeneity of being," the reality of "the other" and its relation to love, and the idea of God as the Creator of Nothingness. Each of these ideas is accompanied by a poem expressing the idea in verse; the idea of love is elaborated in a collection of *Songs to Guiomar*. Apparently the critics of the time were unprepared for this puzzling book, and only in recent years has sufficient attention been devoted to it.

From 1926 onward, Machado also devoted his basic energies to the study, cogitation, and expression of his *Juan de Mairena*, an amorphous but consistently interesting book. The character Juan de Mairena is Machado's ideal of the teacher-sage, a figure like Socrates and the modern Spanish professor which the Free Institute dreamed of producing. Juan de Mairena expresses the accumulated ideas of Machado in a skeptical manner but with an underlying seriousness. The basic Mairena materials were printed piecemeal in the *Diario de Madrid* in 1935, then as a book in 1936. During the Spanish Civil War he continued to add to the book, with increased emphasis on political themes.

In 1927 Machado received an honor normally coveted by the Spanish man of letters when he was elected to the Royal Spanish Academy. It was somewhat ironic that he was to assume the Chair left vacant by the death of José Echegaray, Nobel-prize-winning dramatist, since Machado and his generation scorned Echegaray's works. Somewhat surprisingly, since he had a strong public conscience, Machado waited until 1931 before beginning his speech of acceptance before the Academy; he never got around to finishing it. In a surviving first draft, he chooses in its first words to reveal, although in veiled fashion, his autumn love for Guiomar—a personal reference that undoubtedly would have been lost by the august academicians. As a basic theme he sets out to define poetry, and as usual his ideas are clear and strong. For example, he stresses the fact that for modern man, poetry itself has become a problem, whereas in former periods there was at least a faith in poetry as a cultivated art. He analyzes the important contributions of Marcel Proust and James Joyce, both novelists of course, but for Machado their novels were "degenerated poems." He also attacks the "new poetry" as being poetry of concepts rather than intuition. Machado's discourse trails away at the conclusion; apparently the increasingly revolutionary nature of his political ideas was diminishing his sympathies for the conservative Academy.[21]

In 1931 Machado felt a surge of hope for the political future of his country when the ruling dictator lost power and the monarch Alfonso XIII who supported him was forced to abdicate, and a new Republic was created. As a result, expansive educational programs were begun, especially the creation of new schools. Machado received an appointment to the newly-created Instituto Calderón de la Barca in Madrid. For the first time he became a professor of Spanish literature. But his creative energies were going into his *Juan de Mairena*; his class notebooks (later published against what would have been his wishes) are dry and dull, in marked contrast to the live ideas pulsating in his prose.[22]

Back in Madrid to live after long years of absence, Machado returned to his old habits. He moved into a modest room in the home of his brother José on General Arrando Street, where his mother also lived. After teaching his classes, he always turned up at the Café Español and the *tertulia* there, attended by the painter Ricardo Baroja, brother of the novelist, and the actor Ricardo Calvo, one of his oldest friends. Later the group changed to the Varela Café, but the gathering continued the same, the group sitting quietly, talking sporadically and without much direction. Don Antonio always seemed withdrawn into himself, and as usual his mind was teeming with the ideas of Juan de Mairena. He was also watching the deterioration of the political situation; of course, as he wrote to Guiomar, the intellectual group was becoming disenchanted with the new Republic, struggling to cope with numerous divisive factions.

In the summer of 1936 the whole country was plunged into civil war. Very soon the conflict became international when Germany and Italy sent help for the Nationalist side; Russia and an International Brigade of idealists joined the Loyalist (or Republican) cause. In Spain the Nationalist cause was generally represented by the Church, the Military, and the upper class; the Republican cause by the political liberals, the working class and most of the intellectuals. For the Machado family, as is sometimes the case in civil wars, the Spanish Civil War truly set brother against brother. Antonio's sympathies had always been clearly liberal and Republican; Manuel had gradually showed signs of turning conservative and Nationalist. The outbreak of fighting apparently surprised Manuel while he was visiting in Burgos, a Nationalist city. Undoubtedly after much soul-searching, he declared allegiance to the Nationalist cause, and began to serve by writing poetry as propaganda and by participating in various cultural activities in support of the movement.

Meanwhile, Antonio and the rest of the family remained in Madrid. By November of 1936 the capital was under siege by the Nationalists and the government was moved to Valencia. Antonio was persuaded to go to Valencia also, and his mother joined him. He settled in Rocafort, outside Valencia, and began his wartime task of writing articles for *Hora de España* and *Madrid*, journals published by the Republic. As a public figure, Machado gradually assumed importance. Although he was old and in very poor health, he spoke to a large gathering in Valencia "On the Defense and Diffusion of Culture." His correspondence also became international. There is a letter to David Vigodsky in Leningrad, in which Machado stubbornly refuses to accept the economic emphases of Marxism, but prefers to think of Russia as Tolstoyan, moving toward the ideal of Christian brotherhood. In spite of his official duties, Machado discovered sufficient time and emotion to write a moving sonnet for Guiomar, he near the Mediterranean in Valencia, she near the Atlantic in Portugal, with all Spain between them.

As the political situation worsened for the Loyalists, about a year later the Machados were evacuated to Barcelona, where Antonio continued to write for the Republican cause. A Spanish lady, then an adolescent girl, has retained a vivid memory of exchanging a few words with Don Antonio in a patio in Barcelona; as usual he conveyed an air of quiet kindliness.[23] As late as August, 1938, with the world crashing around him, Machado wrote the prologue for a reprint of one of Valle-Inclán's books, managing to conclude with a few words for the Cause.

In late January, 1939, with the fall of Barcelona imminent,

Antonio Machado and his family joined a small convoy in flight toward the French border.[24] On this journey he was to know the horrors of war directly. There were the usual breakdowns of the vehicles; overnight stays were interminable; the weather was cold and rainy. Although Antonio was himself ill with pneumonia, he had to bear the agony of watching his poor mother, then beyond eighty-five, suffer the same tortures. Finally they arrived in Collioure, a fishing village on the French Mediterranean. Through the month of February Antonio and his mother lay ill, although once he insisted on taking a walk along the seashore. On February 22 he died; his mother perished three days later. Both were buried in the cemetery of Collioure, in the family vault of a friend. Antonio was buried with a brief civil ceremony presided over by his brother José. Manuel, still in Burgos, received the sad news of his brother's death from a complete stranger, who had heard it on the radio. After the war the other brothers left Spain, but Manuel returned to Madrid, was reconverted to Catholicism, and accepted a cultural position granted by the Franco government.

During the later years of his life and after his death, Antonio Machado continued to accumulate honors and tributes of respect both to the man and the poet. In 1932 Soria named him an adopted son, and the poet returned there for an unveiling of a plaque bearing lines of his poetry, which was placed along the road by the Duero where Antonio used to walk. Today in Soria there is an "Antonio Machado Chair" at the Institute; and on the hill where the ruined medieval castle overlooks the Duero River stands the new Antonio Machado National Inn. In 1949, on the tenth anniversary of his death, the journal *Cuadernos hispanoamericanos* of Madrid devoted a double issue to the poet and his work, and in 1960 *Insula* devoted an issue to him. In 1957 the Royal Spanish Academy began a campaign to have the poet's remains returned to his homeland, a campaign still being pursued at the present time. As the passions of the Civil War have gradually receded, Antonio Machado has become one of the honored and honorable figures of Spain and the Hispanic world.

CHAPTER 2

The Poet and the Inner World:
Soledades (Solitudes)

SINCE Antonio Machado gained his enduring reputation as a poet, it is proper that we devote the central chapters of this book to a study of his poetry. The student of Machado's poetry ultimately faces an important decision: whether to approach it from the standpoint of the books themselves, the chronological periods, or the essential themes. Some critics, such as Ricardo Gullón, have stressed the unity of his poetry of four decades; and Ramón de Zubiría organized his fine study, *The Poetry of Antonio Machado*, according to essential themes and symbols.[1] Many critics have followed the natural way of discussing the books themselves, then emphasizing whichever book they felt to be the most important. Earlier critics, such as J. B. Trend and Allison Peers, tended to overemphasize the Machado of *Fields of Castile*, because the Spanish Civil War focused interest on its political themes. We feel strongly that Antonio Machado wrote great poetry in three manners in three fairly well defined periods of his life (and his books tend to follow these periods). Therefore in Chapter 2 we shall concentrate on "The Poet and the Inner World," which completely follows the 1907 *Soledades, galerías y otros poemas* (*Solitudes, Galleries and Other Poems*), and includes his production from 1899-1907. Chapter 3, "The Poet Looks Outward," is largely a study of *Campos de Castilla* (*Fields of Castile*), with a bit of *Nuevas canciones* (*New Songs*), mainly poetry of the years 1907-1917. In Chapter 4, "The Poet as Metaphysician," we have tried to enforce an order upon poetry of quite diverse theme but unified manner, which includes his "Proverbs and Songs" from the previous period.[2] This third period therefore includes poetry from as early as 1912, but mainly that of the Thirties. Within these three chapters, of somewhat comparable length, we hope to indicate the diversity as well as the unity of Machado's poetry; and above all, we shall attempt to prove, as recent criticism of individual books and each period has made apparent, that Machado created outstanding poetry in all three periods.

I *Background of and Influence on* Solitudes, Galleries and Other Poems

In 1907 the publisher Gregorio Pueyo published for Machado an expanded edition of an earlier *Solitudes*, the new version entitled *Solitudes, Galleries and Other Poems*. This edition, which we shall study (and call *Solitudes* for brevity), largely made Machado's reputation as a poet, and he continued to include it, substantially unchanged, in subsequent editions (1917, 1928, 1936, etc.) of his *Poesías completas* (*Complete Poems*). This expanded but selected edition of *Solitudes* in 1907 included all the poetry Machado preferred to preserve of what he had written until that time. We have already seen how young Antonio in the 1890's gradually entered the literary atmosphere of publication and journals in Madrid. By 1898 he was drifting toward poetry; in 1899, according to him, he wrote some of the poems of *Solitudes*. During this period, the poet Juan Ramón Jiménez insists that Machado wrote a youthful book of *Cantares* (*Songs*), which he succeeded in destroying. (Jiménez was annoyed that his own youthful efforts survived.)[3] His first surviving lyrics later were published in the short-lived journal *Electra* in 1901. In late 1902 (and updated 1903) the publisher Antonio Álvarez printed a small collection of Machado's lyrics to the moment, entitled simply *Solitudes*.

This modest volume of some 110 pages contains some of his imperishable lyrics, which he later retouched hardly at all. In general, however, the book is not impressive. Whether through Machado's efforts to destroy them, or because of a small printing, very few copies of the 1903 *Solitudes* survive. In recent years some of the poems have been reprinted, and at least one critic has studied the volume as an integrated book of poems.[4]

Machado, maturing rapidly as a poet in the years after 1903, recognized that many of the poems were diffuse in form and imitative of other poets. He therefore set out to remake the book, discarding some poems, reworking others, and writing new ones more indicative of his own personality. When the 1907 edition of *Solitudes, Galleries and Other Poems* appeared, the earlier edition was forgotten; therefore he has enjoyed the enviable position of having no immature early poetry, the first poem in *Solitudes* (1907) being quite mature.

In spite of Machado's excision of a number of early poems, there remain in *Solitudes* many evidences of the influences of other poets during the years of his apprenticeship. In recent years the literary scholarship has presented this evidence in detail and in depth. Perhaps the most pervasive general influence was that of Gustavo Adolfo Bécquer, also born in Seville, who died in 1870.[5] A Post-Romantic who wrote intimate lyrics during a period when the prevailing poets were realistic or bombastic, Bécquer is generally considered by critics as the first modern Spanish poet. Probably Bécquer was the first poet the young Machado read seriously, and he retained an affection for him all his life.

Machado assimilated much of Bécquer's general philosophy of poetry, as well as some of his specific symbols and images. Central in Bécquer is an idea of poetry as a high ideal impossible to obtain, which he often represents as a fleeing feminine figure. This "disdainful virgin," clad in gauzy tunic and golden sandals, appears with slight variations in the earlier poems of Machado. Bécquer also represented poetry, the unattainable but insistently pursued illusion, as a *corza blanca*, a fleeing white doe. Machado (in poem XLII[6] in *Solitudes*) employs a *corza rápida* with the same meaning, along with an elaborate presentation of the feminine figure as a symbol. As Bécquer's "golden illusion" came under the pressure of a sad and disappointing life, it tended to turn into a chimera; Machado's illusions also took the same descent into chimeras (XXXVI, XLIII, etc.). As a Romantic, Bécquer crashed against the unyielding Realism of the nineteenth century, and as a result often chose the typical refuge, a flight into dreams or a dream-state, thus gaining both protection and separation. Machado very soon *became* the *poeta en sueños*, the poet in reverie; throughout his career, as we shall see, the elaboration of this theme is an outstanding characteristic of his poetry. Machado also followed Bécquer (as did his fellow poet Jiménez) in the creation of the brief, intimate lyric, using often the short traiditional lines such as the octosyllable, with the subtle suggestion provided by assonance rather than complete rhyme. In the later years, Machado refers to Bécquer's poetry as "an accordion played by an angel" (the accordion suggesting the simplicity and intimacy of the music of his poetry), and Bécquer as "the angel of true poetry."[7]

Appearing on the literary scene when he did, Machado could not fail to be influenced somewhat by Rubén Darío. The Nicaraguan poet surprised the literary world with his *Azul* in 1888 and the wildly successful *Prosas profanas* in 1896. Darío, who reintroduced a variety of poetic forms, captivated a whole generation with these exotic and musical lyrics, most of them variations of the erotic theme. Jiménez has confessed how he and Machado around 1902 used to go for walks in the outskirts of Madrid on summer afternoons, "reciting verses of Darío." In the Prologue of *Solitudes*, Machado admits that he "admired the author of *Prosas profanas*, the incomparable master of form and of the senses," but the grave Machado, like his whole generation, shunned even the normally sensual as young men. However, apparently inflamed by one of Darío's most brilliant poems, "Era un aire suave" from *Prosas profanas*, Machado fell under its spell and composed his "Phantasy of an April Night" (LII). Both poems are written in the rare line of *arte mayor*, a twelve-syllable line of balanced hemistichs, very musical if handled properly. In Machado's phantasy, on a Moorish night in Seville the poet is ardently seeking love, but clearly without any confidence, already considering himself an "anachronism." The elegantly musical stanzas finally crumple; the poet thus indicates the crumpling of his hopes for love. Machado, realizing later that the poem did not fit *Solitudes*, nevertheless had not the heart to reject it, and finally decided to hide it away (as it were) in a minor section of the book.

A final strong but very brief influence on the poetry of Machado, which only recently has been clarified, is that of the French poet Paul Verlaine. Late in life, Jiménez remembered that among the Parnassian and Symbolist poets, which as young men they had read avidly, the first was Verlaine, and he recalls specifically that when Machado had returned the copy of *Choix de poèmes* belonging to Jiménez, the edges of the pages were worn out from much reading. A solid article by Geoffrey Ribbans[8] has clarified Machado's specific debt to Verlaine. Machado probably discovered in Verlaine the use of nature to express the poet's own feelings, especially the garden with the fountain. Most of Machado's early poems in the Parnassian manner also have echoes of Verlaine. Moreover, the theme of fatality, especially that expressed by Poe with the adverb "Nevermore," is from Verlaine, not directly from the American poet. It should be made clear, however, that Machado soon began to reveal his own personality and cast off the influence of Verlaine. The French poet, at times frivolous, was, above all, known for his interest in capturing the impressionistic moment; Machado soon became a poet devoted to the power of memory and to the inner light of the soul. In the 1907 *Solitudes*, most of the poems clearly imitative of Verlaine were rejected.

II   *The Two Essential Themes of* Solitudes

That Antonio Machado should call his book *Soledades* has been accepted as so fitting and natural, given his nature, that his choice of title has evoked little comment. In Spanish literature the Golden Age poet Luis de Góngora had appropriated this title for his most famous (or infamous) book, a towering Baroque fragment which is a poetic tour de force that literally stuns the mind, a maze of syntactical and conceptual complexity. While Góngora's *Soledades* was not intimate in the usual sense, nevertheless the aging poet was alleviating his estrangement from life with a poem. Machado apparently was forced to repeat a well-known title simply because it was so pertinent to his own personality. Indeed he and a number of his generation, such as Azorín and Baroja, were solitary men; Azorín himself published a *Soledades* a few years before, but bearing no relation to that of Machado. Moreover, in commenting on this period later, Machado stressed that "The dominant ideology was essentially subjective; art was disintegrating, and the poet . . . pretended only to sing to himself. . ."[9]

Machado's *Solitudes* was his response to this period of subjectivism in his life. In a Prologue written later, he analyzed with his usual clarity and pertinence his aims in the book: "I thought that the poetic element was not the word for its sound values, nor color, nor line, nor a complex of sensations, but a deep palpitation of the spirit." This "deep palpitation of the spirit" became his trademark. He also thought that he could "surprise a few words in intimate monologue, distinguishing the live voice from inert echoes. . ."[10] (As we shall see, he soon rejected the monologue.) While he insists that the two editions of *Solitudes* were in reality "one book," Machado admits that his book was not a "systematic realization" of his aesthetic purposes. We shall have to confess it was not, for no one has succeeded in establishing an entirely convincing organization of *Solitudes*, Machado's own subdivisions being inadequate.

However, the persistent reader of *Solitudes* and some of his later prose finally understands that in general there are two overriding themes which are interrelated. Little by little Antonio Machado himself came to the realization that he was a *poeta en el tiempo*, a poet in time or a poet of time, and that he was also a *poeta en sueños*, a poet of reverie, or memory. In *Solitudes* Machado is a poet of temporality essentially through intuition of time, as is normal in poetry; gradually Machado the philosopher began to analyze the fruits of his intuitions with great clarity. In a defining poem of a single stanza in *Solitudes* (XXXV) he fixes his situation:

> One evening by the wayside we sat down.
> Our life is now time, our sole concern
> The postures of desperation which we assume
> To await. . . . But She that final hour will not spurn.

> *(Al borde del sendero un día nos sentamos.*
> *Ya nuestra vida es tiempo, y nuestra sola cuita*
> *son las desesperantes posturas que tomamos*
> *para aguardar. . . . Mas Ella no faltará a la cita.)*

The lady is of course Death herself, which marks the end of man's temporal existence, but the key phrase is the assertion that "Our life is now time." Machado's intense preoccupation with time is ultimately traceable to his philosophy of life. Machado, as he himself understood, was born into a generation which was the first in Spain to lose the faith in the Church and its promise of eternal life. This loss was critical and profound, and much of the tension in his poetry can be generally traced to the resulting importance attached to temporal existence. Our own Emily Dickinson's personal struggles in her disintegrating Puritan culture provide a meaningful comparable situation. In *Solitudes* Machado projects the temporal theme with his own development of a limited number of traditional symbols: the river, the fountain, the road, etc.

Machado is also the *poeta en sueños*, the poet in dreams. This phrase demands careful definition, much of which the poet himself has provided. To approach a definition from the negative side, he is never referring to the dreams of ordinary sleep, for of course he is too modern to believe in sweet dreams. Nor does he utilize the modern psychological approach to dreams. At this time Freud and his *The Interpretation of Dreams* was unknown to Machado, and even later, when he pursued this type of study, he tended to reject most of Freud's disturbing conclusions. For Machado, to be *en sueños* is a mental state the poet pursued and achieved in his most inspirational waking hours. It is a state of intense reverie, of purposeful daydreaming; the poet looks into his soul and attempts to expand the power of memory, to enhance the remembrance of things past (in Shakespeare's phrase), and in Machado this state usually implies an eternal wait and hope toward the future. In a defining moment he asserts the great importance of this successful exploration of memory (LXXXIX):

> In all of memory the only value is
> The illustrious talent of evoking dreams.
>
> *(De toda la memoria, sólo vale*
> *el don preclaro de evocar los sueños.)*

Quite a number of poems in *Solitudes* emphasize the theme of the power of memory with subtle suggestiveness. This brief lyric (LXXIV), cast in an unobtrusive form of seven- and eleven-syllable lines and with the soft music of assonance, represents a moment of melancholy in the poet's existence:

> Tranquil afternoon, almost
> With placidity of soul . . .
> To be, to have been young

When God was on our side,
To know some joys . . . then distance
And sweetly to remember.

    (Tarde tranquila, casi
con placidez de alma,
para ser joven, para haberlo sido
cuando Dios quiso, para
tener algunas alegrías . . . lejos
y poder dulcemente recordarlas.)

Although the tone of the poem seems impressionistic, actually the last line conveys Machado's special temporal emphasis on memory. While impressionistic poets (such as the early Jiménez) found aesthetic joy in the present moment, it seems that Machado is eager to rush by the experience itself, for the greater pleasure of reelaborating it in his memory.

More typical of the mature Machado is a state of reverie in which there is a confusion of opposing elements. Above all, the reverie is not static; the poet's soul itself is usually "upon the road," in constant, seeking movement.

Upon the bitter earth
My reverie makes roads
That wind like labyrinths, torturous paths,
Parks in bloom, in shadow and in silence;

Deep crypts, and stairways over stars;
Altarpieces of hopes and of remembrances. . .

    (Sobre la tierra amarga,
caminos tiene el sueño
laberínticos, sendas tortuosas,
parques en flor y en sombra y en silencio;

    criptas hondas, escalas sobre estrellas;
retablos de esperanzas y recuerdos. . .) (XXII)

This last line quoted is probably the most powerful and meaningful hendecasyllable Machado ever wrote. In this *retablo* of his mind, Machado, although himself a skeptic, is utilizing the rich suggestiveness of the word *retablo* which refers to the cathedral altarpieces, carved or painted marvels of detail, of beauty, and of religious devotion. The word has also assumed (since Cervantes) the meaning of a backdrop in the puppet theater, and the poet is probably torn between the two meanings of the word. Certainly hopes and remembrances are the two poles of his temporal poetry; Machado is all expanded past and obstinate future of hope.

In another of his much discussed lyrics (LXII), the poet stresses memories by contrasting them with a strong situation of the moment. He first describes the appearance of a summer storm:

> The cloud rent asunder; the rainbow's arc
> Already tinging the sky,
> And a translucent screen of rain
> And sun sweeps over the earth.
>
> *(Desgarrada la nube; el arco iris*
> *brillando ya en el cielo,*
> *y en un fanal de lluvia*
> *y sol el campo envuelto.)*

Unlike the Romantic poets, who would have found immediate inspiration in this strong scene of nature, Machado is only awakened from his poetic reverie, and he asks, "Who disturbs the magic mirrors of my dream?" Briefly then he recaptures his daydreams:

> . . . The lemon trees in bloom,
> The garden's cypress grove,
> Green meadow, sun, water, the rainbow's arch! . . .
> The raindrops in your hair! . . .
>
> *(. . . ¡ El limonar florido,*
> *el cipresal del huerto,*
> *el prado verde, el sol, el agua, el iris! . . .*
> *¡el agua en tus cabellos! . . .*

But the sudden disturbance has shattered his powers of concentration and he returns to reality:

> And everything in memory faded away
> Like tiny bubbles cast upon the wind.
>
> *(Y todo en la memoria se perdía*
> *como una pompa de jabón al viento.)*

As a poet of time and reverie, Machado chose (or his nature chose for him) the late afternoon. The afternoon is the autumn

of the day, and autumn's suggestion of melancholy fitted Machado's temperament. In the quiet time of late afternoon, in the clear light, the poet could evoke his intense reveries. "I go along dreaming roads/ Of the afternoon" begins a typical poem. Or, "It was a clear afternoon, sad and dreamy / Afternoon of summer." Or, "Twilight was falling / Sad and dust-laden." The afternoon is also the time for meditative walks without a particular destination, and Machado's gradual development as a pensive stroller becomes an important factor in his poetry.

The lyrics we have just employed to exemplify the presence of the two central themes in *Solitudes*, time and memory, could be multiplied almost indefinitely, for almost all the poems carry these themes. However, the outstanding lyrics from the extensive collection of *Solitudes* can be profitably organized into four loose groupings on another basis. One group utilizes the memories of childhood; another concerns the poet's search for love and lost youth. In a third and very important group, Machado employs the traditional water symbols to express his temporal preoccupations. Finally, toward the end of *Solitudes*, the poet clearly pauses and doubles back, aware of a new concern, generally ethical and religious. In proceeding, we shall organize our discussion on the basis of these groupings.

III   *The Memories of Childhood*

As a poet of memory explored, intensified, and at times almost created, Machado discovered a special richness in the recollections of childhood. As he began to explore his living past, he gradually settled upon a permanent image, that of the patio in Seville, with its fountain and lemon trees and bright flowers. In general, childhood is transmuted into a time of plenitude, of promise, of innocence and joy, although at times a suggestion of monotony intrudes. Somewhere in his past the poet was touched strongly by the evocative power of children chanting or singing in chorus; thus high-pitched voices must have contrasted sharply against the heavy silence of the old Spanish plazas and houses. In a poem of realistic tone (V), he recalls a schoolroom scene: while a cold rain falls monotonously against the windows, the old schoolmaster thunders corrections at his young students, who are tonelessly chanting the multiplication tables. Presumably the poet was one of the children trapped in the monotony of a scene of droning voices and ceaseless rain.

In a song of marked temporal accent (VIII), Machado evokes the memory of children chanting their songs in the plaza. These songs carry a message of the "sadness of love" and are from "ancient legends." In their innocence, the children are repeating a song of painful experience which they do not understand:

> The children were chanting
> A simple refrain,
> Of something that passes
> And ne'er comes again:
> The story confused
> But clear the pain.

> *(Cantaban los niños*
> *canciones ingenuas,*
> *de un algo que pasa*
> *y que nunca llega:*
> *la historia confusa*
> *y clara la pena.*

In another poem (III), the poet utilizes a memory of the voices and movement of children to contrast the plenitude of this simple existence with his own present sense of loss. He begins by establishing his clear symbol of plenitude, the smiling fruits:

> The plaza and the flaming orange trees
> Laden with their round and smiling fruits.

> *(La plaza y los naranjos escendidos*
> *con sus frutas redondas y risueñas.)*

Into this plaza bursts a tumult of young children just out of school, filling the air with the din of their new-found voices. The poet finds in these sounds an echo of his own past.

> The happiness of childhood in the hidden nooks
>   Of the decaying towns!
> And something of yesterday still ours, that we
> See wandering up and down these ancient streets!

(¡Alegría infantil en los rincones
de las ciudades muertas! . . .
¡Y algo nuestro de ayer, que todavía
vemos vagar por estas calles viejas!)

Perhaps the most imaginative of all Machado's lyrics on the theme of childhood memory is a later one in *Solitudes* called "Dreams" (LXXXII). The poem is composed in traditional stanzas of hendecasyllables, with the subtle music of assonance. The poet uses a variation of his favorite personification, the good-fairies who are sisters, responsible for spinning out his own time and destiny as he imagines it from the beginning. In the opening stanza, one sister spins out a thread which becomes entangled in her sister's spindle:

The fairy of lovely countenance has smiled
On seeing the gleam of a pallid star,
Which in a silken thread, soundless and white,
Entangles in the spindle of her sister fair.

(El hada más hermosa ha sonreído
al ver la lumbre de una estrella pálida
que en hilo suave, blanco y silencioso,
se enrosca al huso de su rubia hermana.)

Then the particular thread of her sister, "the thread of the fields," becomes entangled in her own distaff. Not until the last stanza is the baby introduced whose destiny is connected with these filaments:

The cradle, almost in shadow. The baby sleeps.
The busy fairies sit by the baby's side,
Spinning on their ivory and silver wheels
The subtle filaments of dreams.

(La cuna, casi en sombra. El niño duerme,
Dos hadas laboriosas lo acompañan,
hilandos de los sueños los sutiles
copos en ruecas de marfil y plata.)

Here both the sisters are "fair," but the thread of one is of a "pale star"; the thread of the other, the "thread of earth." Thus there is a blend of both heaven and earth in the baby's destiny.

Surprisingly, in his imagination the poet has gone back in his past beyond the period of effective memory, to babyhood itself. Since Machado's paternal instinct was very weak, we are fairly sure he is imagining his own babyhood, not that of a dreamed-of son. The final emphatic suggestion is that, although the sisters begin by spinning threads of heaven and earth (or promise and reality), in the last stanza both are spinning "threads of dreams," the favorite emotional state of the poet himself.

IV *In Search of Love and Lost Youth*

In *Solitudes*, as the title suggests, we do not expect the plenitude of love, but certainly the poet is blindly and despairingly seeking, and this search creates a painful tension. Indeed, we can say the poet is floundering, hardly beginning to hope for love when he suddenly loses hope. Above all, the poet is a painfully reticent figure; he is surely frightened at normal sensuality. Nevertheless, the desire for love is present, even if it is distant: "Among the golden poplars, / Far off, the shadow of a love awaits" (LXXX). "If I were a poet / of love," he begins once, but the contrary-to-fact clause foredooms the conclusion: he would see in the beloved's eyes "the good and tranquil light" he once saw in his mother's eyes (LXVII).

Once the poet breaks into song and expresses his strongest wishes, and it seems he is about to break out of his shell:

> To create fiestas of love
> In our love we think,
> To burn new incenses
> In distant trackless mountains . . .
>
> *(Crear fiestas de amores*
> *en nuestro amor pensamos,*
> *quemar nuevos aromas*
> *en montes no pisados . . .*

But after this brave start, his continuation indicates that to create these fiestas in "thought" would in fact only cover up the secret of his lack of experience in love. Alone in the park with his musings, he hears a bird hidden in the branches "whistle jestingly"—even nature is laughing at his pretensions. Chagrined, he retreats into the "penumbra of a dream" (XXVII).

Typical also is the image of the poet in the street, eagerly hoping for an appearance of a beloved on the balcony. In one lyric there seems to be promise: "there are echoes of light upon the balconies," perhaps even the fleeting glimpse of a "rose-tinted face." Can it be the one he seeks? "It cannot be," he concludes, and goes on his solitary way in the starlit night (XV). In another lyric strongly reminiscent of Bécquer, the poet is again ready for love: "Life today has the rhythm / of waves . . ." (XLII). The imagined lass proves to be disdainful; nevertheless the poem ends on a note of hopeful expectation: "Let the golden arrow / Tremble in my breast."

In *Solitudes* the beloved never quite becomes a figure of flesh and blood, and indeed Machado soon transmutes the feminine figures into symbolic ones. In "Gallant's Inventory" (XL), the feminine figures have become sisters. The one is a dark, seductive lass, even a "gypsy" type, whose "Dark flesh" reminds the poet of "Sun-kissed wheat." The poet has a desire to seek out this lass of passion, but makes clear that she represents temporality and will leave only a song of ashes on his lips. The poet is then more permanently attracted to her sister, who is fragile and fair, "A morning star / In the blue distances." For this fair maiden, who of course represents the permanence of the ideal, he will take the tenderest flowers of the white almond blossoms and make her a "tiny white bouquet." In this lyric Machado subtly interweaves the description of the sisters, the repetition of the image of the morning star, and the musicality of the assonance.

Machado utilizes again the personification of the two sisters in what is perhaps his finest song in *Solitudes* (XXXVIII). It begins as a springtime song, of beauty and of promise.

> April was in bloom
> Beyond my windowpane.
> Upon a balcony,
> Bedecked with flaming jasmine
> And with white-tinted roses,
> Two sisters could be seen.
> The younger plied her needle,
> The older spinning was . . .

> *(Abril florecía*
> *frente a mi ventana.*
> *Entre los jazmines*
> *y las rosas blancas*
> *de un balcón florido*
> *vi las dos hermanas.*
> *La menor cosía,*
> *la mayor hilaba . . .)*

The presence of the loom, of spinning and sewing, of course suggests that the sisters are spinning out the poet's time and fate. In this song, each of the sisters has a distinct symbolic meaning. The younger is "smiling and rosy-faced," and probably represents sorrow or sadness. The poet soon makes it obvious that his theme is not the conflict between joy and melancholy. In the second stanza, after some time has passed, the poet begins a dialogue with the older sister, now weeping alone on the balcony, who silently shows him the garment the two were making before:

> She held aloft the garment
> The younger had begun.
> In the black tunic's folds
> The silver needle shone . . .
>
> She looked at the afternoon
> Of April that was dreaming,
> While from a distant tower,
> The sound of bells was streaming.

> *(Señaló el vestido*
> *que empezó la hermana.*
> *En la negrá tunica*
> *la aguja brillaba . . .*
>
> *Señaló a la tarde*
> *de abril que soñaba,*
> *mientras que se oía*
> *tañer de campanas.)*

In the third part of the song, after another lapse of time, on another placid afternoon, the poet is again before the balcony bedecked with flowers, now significantly deserted. Both of the sisters are gone, and on the loom the linen thread is being spun by an "invisible hand." And at this point, the poet introduces one of his important images, that of the mirror: "And in the darkened room/ The moon of the limpid mirror/Was gleaming." He repeats the image of the mirror in the conclusion:

> Among the white tuberoses
> And the flaming jasmine
> Of the balcony hung with flowers,
> I looked upon my face
> In the clear moon of the mirror
> That in the distance was dreaming . . .

> *(Entre los jazmines*
> *y las rosas blancas*
> *del balcón florido,*
> *me miré en la clara*
> *luna del espejo*
> *que lejos soñaba . . .)*

Machado uses the mirror as a part of his soul in his process of memory. When it is reflecting properly, it gives him the reflection of reality, a meaningful consciousness based on the power of memory, recreated and poetically amplified. Thus the presence of the limpid mirror indicates that he has lost the sisters of joy and sorrow, his life has lost feeling and meaning. Moreover, normally his mirror is close within his soul; here it is detached and far away. Although April is still blooming, the poet on looking in the mirror sees only himself, lost in the hopeless solitude, the black despair of feeling that his very soul is failing to function. This song, virtually impossible to translate adequately, is one of Machado's finest examples of poetic suggestion.

Machado treats the theme of lost passion for life in another poem, which has justly become an anthology piece (XI). In addition to the main theme, he also utilizes very effectively the theme of the "road." The poem begins with one of the essential Machadian lines:

> I go along dreaming roads
> In the afternoon. The hills
> Of golden hue, the verdant pines,
> The oaks laden with dust!
> Where will the roadway wind?

> *(Yo voy soñando caminos*
> *de la tarde. ¡Las colinas*
> *doradas, los verdes pinos,*
> *las polvorientes encinas! . . .*
> *¿Adónde el camino irá?*

It is the poet's time, the promising afternoon, and the soul seems ready for adventure. But, as usual, he is plagued by the pressure of the past, when he had a love, but the torment of it drove him to seek escape.

> I make my way in song, wayfarer
> Upon an endless way . . .
> —Evening is overtaking day—
> "Within my heart I had a thorn
>   Of passion true and real;
> One day I snatched it out in scorn:
>   My heart now nothing feels."
>
> *(Yo voy cantando, viajero*
> *a lo largo del sendero . . .*
> *—La tarde cayendo está—*
> *"En el corazón tenía*
> *la espina de una passión;*
> *logré arrancármela un día:*
> *ya no siento el corazón.")*

During a moment of relief the poet is soothed by the somber quiet of the countryside. But his soul needs movement, a road on which to wander to be functioning; yet looking out upon the darkening evening, he sees his very road fade away: "And the road that twists and winds / Is lost in darkness and disappears." The poet has thus the intuition that pain and passion are inseparable, that anything is preferable to a soul devoid of feeling, and he pleads for the return of pain.

> My song becomes a plaint again:
> "Could I but feel once more
> The sharp but golden thorn thrust deep
> Within my heart's core."
>
> *(Mi cantar vuelve a plañir:*
> *"Aguda espina dorada,*
> *quién te pudiera sentir*
> *en el corazón clavada.")*

As Machado continues to explore both past and present in his quest of love, he becomes increasingly disillusioned. In evoking his memories, he is likely to discover mainly childhood memories. His stock of memories of mature love is woefully poor; therefore even intense elaboration and re-creation will yield only meager results. And as he stands yearningly before the balconies, he is doomed to defeat almost before he has begun. Thus he begins to dwell upon the realization that his youth, the proper time for love, has passed irrevocably, though he is in fact still a young man. At the end of the poem "Perhaps" (L), after presenting again all the details of promising spring, he records "declamatorily" (like an old man) his conclusion, still with the faintest of hopes:

> "How late it now is for my happiness!"
> And then, upon my way like one who feels
> The wings of another illusion:—And still to say,
> "I vow I'll catch up to my youth one day!"

> *(—¡Cuán tarde ya para la dicha mía!—*
> *Y luego, al caminar, como quien siente*
> *alas de otra illusión:—Y todavía*
> *¡yo alcanzaré mi juventud un día!)*

But this weak hope goes unrealized, as another poem on the same theme indicates (XLIII). The poet begins (unusual for Machado) in the smiling promise of an April morning, with its soft odors and fountain laughter and lark songs. But he soon shifts to his "clear afternoon of melancholy," with its tolling bells. Although the poem is cast in the strongly musical dodecasyllables, which the *modernistas* preferred for melodious effects, the conclusion could not be more somber or final:

> I asked the dying April afternoon:
> "Is happiness at last come to my house?"
> The afternoon of April smiled: "Happiness
> Passed by your door," and added somberly:
> "It passed your door. It never passes twice."

> *(Pregunté a la tarde de abril que moría:*
> *"¿Al fin la alegría se acerca a mi casa?"*
> *La tarde de abril sonrió: "La alegría*
> *pasó por tu puerta"—y luego, sombría:*
> *"Pasó por tu puerta. Dos veces no pasa.")*

V   *The Symbols of Flowing Water*

In *Solitudes* perhaps the poems which evoke the deepest response in our consciousness are those which utilize the water symbols. In his earliest poems Antonio Machado showed a propensity toward the ancient water symbols, and his struggle in *Solitudes* is to capture and express his personal variations around these traditional materials. Later he was to discover the ancient source of the water symbolism in the fragments of the philosopher Heraclitus, who found in the flowing river the idea that change and flow were the eternal things.

As for the symbol of the fountain, Machado apparently first became conscious of it in his reading of Symbolist poets such as Verlaine, but in his earliest poems he is somewhat unsure of what it means to him. In one of the fine lines of "The Fountain,"[11] he declares, "I adored the symbols of water and of stone," and goes on to confess: "Thus far I cannot comprehend the magic / Sounds of water . . ." For the youthful poets (Machado was young at the time) the waters fell with a "frivolous, erotic murmur." But rejecting this normal reaction, Machado focuses on the paradox of the double eternity "of water and stone," the former suggesting the changeable, the latter the permanent. In this poem the fountain thus remains a "mystery." Later, Machado unjustly discarded this fine poem from *Solitudes*, apparently because he felt it to be imitative.

At a propitious time in his poetic development, Machado made what was apparently his first visit to Seville and the old palace where he was born. In the fine patio of the palace, a source of his richest childhood memories, he seized upon the flowing fountain there as his own fountain symbol, specific and personal, and now permanent in his consciousness. In the enthusiasm of his rediscovery, he put in his poem the natural evidences of a poet's revisiting his birthplace. Realizing soon that such personal notes were youthful romanticism, he deleted all personal reference in the final version in *Solitudes* (VII). In the dreamy opening lines, he focuses upon the interrelation of two basic symbols, the fruits and the fountain:

> The lemon tree languidly suspends
> A pale, dust-laden branch

> Above the enchantment of the limpid fountain,
> And in its shimmering depths
> The golden fruits are dreaming . . .

> *(El limonero lánguido suspende*
> *una pálida rama polvorienta*
> *sobre el encanto de la fuente limpia,*
> *y allá en el fondo sueñan*
> *los frutos de oro. . . .)*

The poet has come, seeking the "candid illusion," but his intuition tells him differently. In the clarity of his mind, he thinks "nevermore," though his heart stubbornly trusts in a future:

> In the atmosphere of fading afternoon
> That aroma of absence floats
> Which tells the illumined spirit: Nevermore,
> And tells the heart: Wait.

> *(En el ambiente de la tarde flota*
> *ese aroma de ausencia*
> *que dice al alma luminosa: nunca,*
> *y al corazón: espera.)*

He has already lost the illusions of childhood, which he has little hope of recovering. Significant is his shift to the past tense, when with his mother's encouragement he could actually grasp the fruits; when he returns to the present the fruits have become "dream," their only reality being the reality of memories:

> For you once saw me plunge my innocent hands
> Into the waters serene,
> And reach the enchanted fruits
> That today in the depths of the fountain dream.

> *(Que tú me viste hundir mis manos puras*
> *en el agua serena,*
> *para alcanzar los frutos encantados*
> *que hoy en el fondo de la fuente sueñan. . .)*

In a song commented upon above (VII), Machado is still struggling to establish his mature symbolic meaning for the fountain. Although the melancholy outpouring of the "old cadences" of the children is the central element of the lyric, the poet also introduces as a parallel element a "fountain serene" whose ceaseless flow tells a story of forgotten details but remembered pain:

> Its legend continued
> The fountain serene;
> The story obscured,
> It told of the pain.

> *(Seguía su cuento*
> *la fuente serena;*
> *borrada la historia,*
> *contaba la pena.)*

In a major poem of *Solitudes* (VI), Machado develops with mature intuition the theme of the flowing fountain as a symbol of time and memory. As usual, he chooses his typical time of day: "It was a clear afternoon, a sad and dreamy afternoon of summer." In the park, he is attracted inevitably to the fountain:

> Within the solitary park, the sonorous
> And bubbling murmur of the water's melody
> Led me to the fountain. The fountain streamed
> Upon the marble white its monotony.

> *(En el solitario parque, la sonora*
> *copla borbollante del agua cantor*
> *me guió a la fuente. La fuente vertía*
> *sobre el blanco mármol su monotonía.)*

Then the poet breaks into an intimate dialogue with the fountain, a dialogue that gradually reveals his temporal preoccupations.

> The fountain was singing: "Brother, does my song
> Of present moment recall a distant dream?"
> It was a lazy afternoon of slow summer.

> I responded to the fountain:
> "Sister, I remember not,
> But I know well your present tune is remote."

> *(La fuente cantaba:—¿Te recuerda, hermano,*
> *un sueño lejano mi canto presente?*
> *Fue una tarde lenta del lento verano.*

Respondí a la fuente: –
No recuerdo, hermana,
mas sé que tu copla presente es lejana.)

The fountain then reminds the poet how in the past time was full, time was complete; there was a possibility of fruitful loves and fond hopes. The poet begs the fountain with its "enchanted voice" to revive for him again "the happy forgotten legends." But the fountain now knows no such legends:

"I know no legends of ancient happiness,
Now only withered stories of loneliness.

It was a clear afternoon of lazy summer . . .
You came, my brother, alone with your pain
Your lips touched in kiss my waters serene,
They told your pain those clear afternoons."

(– Yo no sé leyendas de antigua alegría,
sino historias viejas de melancolía.

   Fue una clara tarde del lento verano . . .
Tú venías solo con tu pena, hermano;
tus labios besaron mi linfa serena,
y en la clara tarde, dijeron tu pena.)

This sad and monotonous reply of course does not satisfy the poet, who departs in worsened isolation:

"Farewell for always, ever-sounding fountain,
Eternal songstress of the quiet parks.
Farewell forever, your eternal monotony
Is sadder, fountain, than this pain of mine."

(– Adiós para siempre, la fuente sonora,
del parque dormido eterna cantora.
Adiós para siempre; tu monotonía,
fuente, es más amarga que la pena mía.)

Here Machado has very successfully followed Verlaine's famous dictum, "Music above all else," to leave an enduring suggestion of theme. He repeats with subtle variation the melodious line of the clear summer afternoon almost as a refrain. The subtly varied but very heavy rhymes (difficult to reproduce in translation) contribute also to the seductive effects. Moreover, there is a suggestive intimacy in the brother-sister dialogue with the fountain. The murmuring of the fountain, which now means to the poet the eternal melancholy of time lost, keeps echoing in our consciousness long after we have finished reading the poem.

Usually Machado's fountain is streaming time, a painful though necessary flowing which tells the poet his soul is alive, but at least once he achieves a very fine poem by emphasizing the interrupted flow. The elements of the brief lyric are entirely simple:

> The embers of a purple twilight fume
> Beyond the darkling grove of cypress trees . . .
> Inside the shadowed bower stands the fountain,
> With its winged and naked Love-god of stone
> Now mutely dreaming. In the marble basin
> Lie the waters dead.
>
> *(Las ascuas de un crepúsculo morado*
> *detrás del negro cipresal humean . . .*
> *En la glorieta en sombra está la fuente*
> *con su alado y desnudo Amor de piedra,*
> *que sueña mudo. En la marmórea taza*
> *reposa el agua muerta.)*

As we have seen, the streaming embers of a sunset, with a touch of color and suggested movement, would usually serve to intensify the activity in the poet's soul, his sense of living. But here he proceeds with images of unusual quietness and stillness—the dark grove, the shadowy bower, and the smooth immobility of stone and marble. Then all the contrast is concentrated in the truncated last line; the suggestion of lifelessness falls heavily (in Spanish) on the phonetic quality of the word *muerta*. There is a stifling finality which keeps echoing in our consciousness after we finish the poem. We expect the fountain to be streaming, but it is not. And the poet's very soul is frozen in the immobility of the waters.

In addition to the fountain, Machado early and firmly seized upon the ancient water symbol of the river as a means of emphasizing the temporal in poetry. Even in his childhood studies he must have learned from memory some of the stanzas of Jorge Manrique's famous "Stanzas on the Death of His Father," written in the fifteenth century. Manrique actually expanded his specific elegiac theme to such an extent that the poem has become the classic expression of the medieval Spanish Catholic philosophy of life, a philosophy which prevailed in Spain up to Machado's generation. In the 1903 *Solitudes*, Machado placed as the final poem a "Gloss" of one of the key sentences of Manrique's elegy.

> Our lives are rivers flowing down
> Unto the sea, which sea is death.

For writing the all-encompassing lines, says Machado, Manrique has a special altar among his favorite poets. We hasten to add that Machado as a twentiety-century poet gradually extended a meaning that the medieval Catholic poets did not have. In stressing the inexorable flow of this life down to death, Manrique is by contrast making the later eternal life infinitely greater. For the medieval mind, of course, there was no contradiction in thinking of the body as temporal and the soul in that body as eternal. For Machado, however, the "Blind flight down to the sea" was fraught with possibilities of ultimate annihilation, a possibility he has premonitions of, but of course never completely tries to resolve in this period.

Since Machado's gloss of one of Manrique's sentences is obviously imitative, in one of the longest and most essential poems of *Solitudes* he returns to a development of the river symbol (XIII). His setting is what came to be his typical one, the poet on the road:

> Toward a radiant sunset,
> The summer sun was wending,
> Gigantic trumpet among the flame-streaked clouds,
> Behind green poplars along the river banks . . .
>
> I went along my road,
> Absorbed in the lonely country twilight.

> *(Hacia un ocaso radiante*
> *caminaba el sol de estío,*
> *y era, entre nubes de fuego, una trompeta gigante,*
> *tras de los álamos verdes de las márgenes del río . . .*
>
> *Yo iba haciendo mi camino*
> *absorto en el solitario crepúsculo campesino.*

For a moment, the poet is lulled by the scene and he breaks into an unrestrained lyrical expression of optimism:

I thought: "Lovely afternoon, celestial music notes
All disdain and harmony,
Fair afternoon, you cure the melancholy
Of this vain darkling corner that thinks!"

*(Y pensaba: "¡Hermosa tarde, nota de lira inemensa
toda desdén y armonía;*
*hermosa tarde, tú curas la pobre melancolía
de este rincón vanidoso, oscuro rincón que piensa!")*

But the sound and movement of the flowing river awaken the poet's old preoccupations, his sense of temporality:

I made my weary road,
Feeling the ancient anguish that makes a heavy heart.

The somber waters passed in their melancholy way
Beneath the curving arches,
As if in passing to say:
"No sooner, O wayfarer,
Is the bark cast off from its mooring tree,
It sings: We nothing are.
Where the poor river ends, awaits the boundless sea."

Beneath the bridge's arches, the somber waters passed.
(I thought: this soul of mine!)

I paused a moment more
In the evening to meditate . . .
What is this drop upon the wind
That cries out to the sea, I am the sea? . . .
I, in the dusty afternoon,
Turned back toward the town.

The buckets continued creaking on the somnolent waterwheel.
Beneath the somber branches, the waters were tumbling down.

(Yo caminaba cansado,
sintiendo la vieja angustia que hace el corazón pesado.

El agua en sombra pasaba tan melancólicamente,
bajo los arcos del puente,
como si al pasar dijera:

"Apenas desamarrada
la pobre barca, viajero, del árbol de la ribera,
se canta: no somos nada.
Donde acaba el pobre río la inmensa mar nos espera."

Bajo los ojos del puente pasaba el agua sombría.
(Yo pensaba: ¡el alma mía!)

Y me detuve un momento,
en la tarde, a meditar . . .
¿Qué es esta gota en el viento
que grita al mar: soy el mar? . . .

Yo, en la tarde polvorienta,
hacia la ciudad volvía.
Sonaban los cangilones de la noria soñolienta.
Bajo las ramas oscuras caer el agua se oía.)

Again Machado has concentrated his emphasis on the central symbol of the water, this time the flowing river. Obviously he has returned to Manrique's symbol, with his own intense concern. He feels the journey of the "bark" of the soul to be only a moment; then his intuition tells him that all is nothingness. Here the "boundless sea" is first death, but in the next stanza it becomes the universal consciousness. Machado does not have the Christian faith in the eternal nature of the soul: for him it is blind arrogance to be sure that the "drop upon the wind" of the soul is of the same substance as God. Still the poet can at least assert the possibility; more and more Machado was to stress, however, the problem of the soul's contact with God and even the nature of God.

In the poem under discussion, Machado introduced another water symbol, that of the Moorish waterwheel. In another section of *Solitudes* called "Humor, Phantasies, Notes," he concentrates upon the waterwheel along with the symbol of the poor mule who goes round and round to turn the wheel and lift the water. Machado's increasing skepticism drove him to this humor, but it is unusual in this book, always a low-keyed and anguished humor. In this poem (XLVI), the poet, again on a late dust-laden afternoon, begins with the continuous sound of the water in the buckets of the waterwheel. But he prefers to concentrate on the plight of the poor old mule chained to this monotonous round.

The mule was lost in dreams,
Poor mule going around,
Moved by the somber rhythm
That in the water sounds.

I know not what poet,
Touched by divine zeal,

Joined to the painfulness
Of the eternal wheel
The flowing harmony
Of water steeped in dream,
And covered up your eyes,
Poor old animal!

> *(Soñaba la mula,*
> *¡pobre mula vieja!,*
> *al compás de sombra*
> *que en el agua sueña.*
>
> *Yo no sé que noble,*
> *divino poeta, . . .*
> *unió a la amargura*
> *de la eterna rueda*
> *la dulce armonía*
> *del agua que sueña*
> *y vendó tus ojos*
> *¡pobre mula vieja!)*

With the sound and movement of the waterwheel as a strong time symbol, surely the unseeing old donkey is a symbol of humanity, condemned actively to suffer. Not only must man see himself fade into nothingness in a few hours, but he also invents contraptions which emphasize the inexorable passage of those hours. Therefore, says the poet ironically, the inventor of the waterwheel must have been a poet, a poet with a "heart mature in somberness and in science."

VI   *In the Galleries of the Soul*

In his searching and questioning, toward the end of *Solitudes*, Machado sits down one day and reads the poems he has formerly written. In them he finds that a "divine truth, / Trembling with fear," is waiting to burst forth. By looking inward, into the bottomless "galleries of remembrance," the poet can discover the essentials of life. This "gallery" (*galería*), which is Machado's symbol of the soul, is understood to be a closed space, possibly immense, into whose immensity the windows let in the light, often as from a distance. As a part of his discovered truth the poet has realized the inevitability of human suffering: "Today you'll seek in vain / Consolation for your pain" (XIX). Moreover, his "Gallery of remembrance," his reverie, now becomes attached

to an "eternal labor"; the poet is now a laborer instead of a singer. He will now "dream" to a serious purpose, and his symbol
for this labor is the beehive—"We work a new honey /With the
old griefs." Actually Machado has been working in the gallery of
the soul before in *Solitudes*, so that there is only a shift of emphasis from the aesthetic to the ethical and religious.

In the section of "Galleries," two lyrics which are companion
pieces (LXIII and LXIV) provide the beginning of a transition
from the aesthetic to the religious. Both have been quoted ex-
tensively by critics as very typical of Machado. The direct influence upon both poems is probably that of Bécquer. Although as
a Romantic poet Bécquer's primary theme was love, in a few intense lyrics he explored the depths of his soul. In his poem
Rima XLVII, when he looks down into the bottomless chasm of
a human heart, both his eyes and his soul are disquieted, because
"How deep it was, and dark."

This manner of looking inward, of attempting to feel the deep
palpitation of the soul, is essential in Machado. In the first of
his two poems (LXIII), like Bécquer the poet sees the darker
side of things: in "the deep crypt of the soul" there awaits the
"demon" of his dream. Although "the fairest of angels," this
demon grasps the frightened poet's hand and forces him onward:

> "You must come down with me." And I advanced
> Into my dream, stunned by the reddish glare;
> And in the crypt I felt the sounding chains
> Of hosts of caged beasts stirring there.

> *(—Vendrás conmigo ... Y avancé en mi sueño,*
> *cegado por la roja luminaria.*
> *Y en la cripta sentí sonar cadenas*
> *Y rebullir de fieras enjauladas.)*

Of course these caged beasts are the dark aggressions and
furious passions (the Freudian elements) in the human soul, but
at this stage in his career Machado is too reticent to do more
than suggest dark presences.

The second lyric (LXIV) is more typical of the Machado of
Solitudes. Again a voice calls out to him "from the threshold of
a dream," but this time it is "the good, the beloved voice." And
when the poet is invited to behold his soul, he follows with
confidence:

"With you always." And in my dream I advanced
Down through a long, deserted gallery
Feeling the rustle of her garments pure
And the gentle quiver of her loving hand.

(—Contigo siempre . . . Y avancé en mi sueño
por una larga, escueta galería,
sintiendo el roce de la veste pura
y el palpitar de la mano amiga.)

From other poems we suspect that this "loving hand" is still the memory of that of his mother. As we have seen in an earlier section, however, the poet has hopes that this feminine hand will become that of the beloved, and, by further sublimation, the symbol of the good and the inspirational. While both these lyrics, typical of the Symbolist manner, are still largely aesthetic, there is a suggestion of his new preoccupation with the ethical in phrases such as the "good voice."

Surely the poem which most adequately expresses Machado's triumphs and failures at this point is "Last Night as I Lay Sleeping" (LXIX).[12] The form of the poem is perfect, with three tightly woven stanzas carefully rhymed, one for each symbol used. The initial lines suggest the tradition of Spanish mystic poetry:

Last night as I lay sleeping,
I dreamed—Oh illusion blest!—
There was a fountain flowing
Deep down inside my breast.

(Anoche cuando dormía
soñé, ¡bendita illusión!,
que una fontana fluía
dentro de mi corazón.)

The second stanza commences with the same structure (in the manner of an essential, insistent refrain), but introduces another important symbol:

Last night when I lay sleeping,
I dreamed—Oh illusion blest!—
There was a beehive working
Deep down inside my breast . . .

(Anoche cuando dormía
sone, ¡bendita illusión!

> *que una colmena tenía*
> *dentro de mi corazón . . .)*

As a critic has recently suggested,[13] probably Machado was consciously following in a general way certain writings of St. Theresa. As a mystic who experienced mysticism in both its contemplative and active aspects, St. Theresa expressed herself by utilizing the fountain (as the life source itself, ultimately God) and the hive (the laborer dispensing fraternal charity). In the third stanza, Machado develops the symbol of the sun as light, another of the basic mystic symbols, and a favorite of St. John of the Cross, whom Machado admired as a poet. Thus this whole poem is steeped in the mystic tradition, and has at times been interpreted as such in Spanish criticism. But in his final stanza the poet subtly but clearly suggests his own longings and limitations:

> Last night when I lay sleeping
> I dreamed—Oh illusion blest!—
> That it was God I had
> Deep down inside my breast.

> *(Anoche cuando dormía*
> *soñé, ¡bendita ilusión!,*
> *que era Dios lo que tenía*
> *dentro de mi corazón.)*

The soothing rhythms of the poem should not deceive us as to the sense of the stanza. In the Christian mystics, after intense preparation through the stages of purgation and illumination, in the stage of union the soul comes to *know* God directly. Here, not only is the poet *dreaming* that he had found God, but even in this dream it is also an illusion, however blessed the moment.

This mood of anguish deepens in a poem which follows (LXXVII). Whereas before the poet dreamed on the "clear afternoon," now even his favorite time has darkened and lost its former magic:

> It is an ash-gray, gloomy afternoon,
> Bedraggled like my poor soul;
> And there is this old anguish
> That feeds the hypochondria I always feel.

> The causes of this anguish I grasp not,
> Nor even vaguely can I comprehend;

But I have memory, and remembering say,
"Yes, I was a child, and you were my good friend."

(Es una tarde cenicienta y mustia,
destartalada, como el alma mía;
y es esta vieja angustia
que habita mi usual hipocondría.

La causa de esta angustia no consigo
ni vagamente comprender siquiera;
pero recuerdo y, recordando, digo;
—Sí, yo era niño, y tú, mi compañera.)

Before he was a poet of melancholy, then grief and pain; now
he is a poet of anguish. He goes on to compare himself to a
homeless dog lost on the roads and to a child lost among the
noise and confusion of a night of fiesta, finally to conclude:

Thus I go along, a melancholy drunk,
Moonstruck guitarist, poet:
Alas, poor John-o-dreams,
Forever seeking God among the mists.

(Así voy yo, borracho melancólico,
guitarrista lunático, poeta,
y pobre hombre en sueños,
siempre buscando a Dios entre la niebla.)

The anguished cry in the last line is the first direct statement of
his religious hunger. Years later he was to insist that in this
poem there is a poetic intuition of the existential anguish of
Heidegger.[14]

From this point, his very inspiration is threatened, for the
human pain which before provided substance for his poetic
labor is now overwhelming him. In LXXXVI he begins by saying that yesterday his human griefs were like silkworms, spinning
out their threads, or that before his pains brought "good tears"
which refreshed the garden of his inspiration. But today all
that is changed:

The human pains that yesterday
Made of my heart a hive
Today are treating my poor heart
Like an ancient wall:
They want to tumble down the stones
And soon to have it fall.

*(Dolores que ayer hicieron
de mi corazón colmena,
hoy tratan mi corazón
como a una muralla vieja:
quieren derribarlo, y pronto,
al golpe de la piqueta.)*

Antonio Machado ends his poetic venture in *Solitudes* with a confession of defeat, a failure which fortunately proved to be only temporary. In the penultimate lyric, significantly called "Mundane Stanzas" (XCV) the poet has returned, not to the profane or common, but to the world of prose reality, the realm of the philosopher.

A poet yesterday, poor gimlet-eyed
Philosopher today;
I have exchanged for copper pennies
The gold of yesterday.

*(Poeta ayer, hoy triste y pobre
filósofo trasnochado,
tengo en monedas de cobre
el oro de ayer cambiado.)*

Generally he means that he has exchanged the gold of poetic intuition for the copper of rational ideas, of philosophy. Specifically, he has lost irrevocably the "gold" of youth, the inspiration that came from the emotion of smiles and tears. At least he has freed himself of the *mal de amor* that is able to weep without pain; today when he looks into his "galleries of remembrance" he can only create "Alleluyas of disconsolate / Elegies of yesterday." These elegies are of course concerned with his essential theme, the irreversibility of time. Later he was to formalize the theme of this poem, declaring that the poet is fated to oscillate between philosophy and poetry, between idea and intuition.

VII   *Conclusion*

In summary, Antonio Machado's *Solitudes, Galleries and Other Poems* has attained a position of primary importance in Spanish literature, both as an example of renovation in poetry and as an enduring achievement based on the emphases of that renovation. During Machado's formative years, Spanish poetry was in a marked state of decline, tending toward the prosaic philosophical grousings of a Campoamor or the outmoded civil preoccupations of a Núñez de Arce. Machado's fellow poet Juan Ramón Jiménez, at the end of his long career, made a ringing statement which no one has disputed: "It fell to Machado and to me to initiate in our modern poetry the expression of the inner spirit (*lo interior*)."[15] Even the modest Machado gave himself a high place for his expression of *intimismo*,[16] the innermost, the intimate (and by intimate he assuredly does not mean frank confession). Machado also pointed out with pride that, in anticipation of the new aesthetics in modern poetry, "*Solitudes* was the first Spanish book form which was totally proscribed the anecdotal,"[17] because in the 1907 edition he deleted all personal reference and episode.

The poems of *Solitudes* reflect that "deep palpitation of the spirit" which became a permanent characteristic of Antonio Machado. Many of the lyrics seem to begin in the Impressionistic manner, with a finely expressed effect of nature reflected in the poet's soul, but the aim is not primarily aesthetic. In *Solitudes*, Machado is by technique a Symbolist poet, working and reworking a few essential symbols, the gallery, the road, the fountain, the river, etc. By intuition at this point, Machado is a poet of marked temporality. Harking back to a direction of Romanticism as exemplified partly in Bécquer, Machado is also a *poeta en sueños*, a poet of memory, evoking, elaborating, and re-creating the past, and pondering hopefully over the future. This preoccupation with time and the method of prolonging it through memory becomes an obsession, and by intuition in *Solitudes* he actually becomes an Existentialist poet, although Existentialism as a movement is not defined until later. *Solitudes* begins in faint hope and ends in confused (but temporary) defeat, the poet's becoming "philosopher." But the simple poems themselves strike a profound chord in the consciousness of the reader. Many of the imperishable lines, such as "I go along dreaming roads / In the afternoon," have become a permanent addition to the Spanish literary heritage.

CHAPTER 3

The Poet Looks Outward:
Campos de Castilla (Fields of Castile)

WHEN Antonio Machado published the first version of *Fields of Castile* in 1912, he earned membership in the famous Generation of 98, which indeed received at about this time its definitive name by Azorín. The publication of this edition proved to be premature, however, for in a preliminary *Complete Poems* of 1917, Machado added a significant number of poems to the original *Fields of Castile*. Even in *Nuevas canciones* (*New Songs*) of 1924, a number of poems show a continuity of themes of *Fields of Castile*. Therefore we have preferred in our discussion to concentrate on three themes important to the poet during roughly the years 1905-1924. The first group of poems deals with the theme of the problem and destiny of Spain, generally called the Castilian theme, and of course includes the Soria poems as typical of Castile. The second group are *elogios*, or poems in praise of those Machado considered worthy cultural figures, and a type of poem he sought to establish a first-class status for. The third group traces the history of the poet's love for Leonor in Soria, the shock of the loss of that love, and the persistence and the problems of the memories of it. Admittedly this selection of themes leaves out a fairly important group of songs, *coplas*, and lyrics generally imitations of popular forms (CLIX, etc.). And we have chosen to discuss the extensive sections of "Proverbs and Songs," some written as early as 1909, with the poetry of the later period.

I *The Background of* Fields of Castile

Antonio Machado has come to be called the poet of the Generation of 98 on the strength of his Castilian poems. But to put this appellation in proper perspective, certain problems must be clarified. The term Generation of 98 has become a critic's phrase to designate a historical group especially concerned with the specific problem of the destiny of Spain. Therefore, the Nobel Prize-winning poet Juan Ramón Jiménez, who began to publish even before Machado, has never been considered to be of the Generation of 98 because he preferred not to write on the Spanish theme. Moreover, a few critics have excluded Machado himself from the Generation, because of the late date at which he began to write on the Castilian theme. The charter members of the Generation were, as Luis Granjel has demonstrated, Unamuno, José Martínez Ruiz (Azorín), Pío Baroja, and a figure less well-known today, Ramiro de Maeztu. Certainly Granjel correctly designates Machado as an epigonic member, since he joined the group late.[1] Machado actually became the poet of the Generation by fortuitous circumstances; Unamuno earned his fame as an essayist and philosopher, and Azorín, Baroja, and Maeztu (surprisingly for Spaniards) simply never wrote poetry.

Earlier in the biographical chapter, we stressed the fact that around 1905 Machado, strongly influenced by the personality and writings of Unamuno, turned away from the aesthetic and personal concerns of *Solitudes* and began to forge himself a new life. He undoubtedly studied with care the essential essays of Unamuno. As early as 1895, Unamuno published a series of essays under the general title *En torno al casticismo*, concerned with an extensive analysis of the essential Spanish character, and the special contribution of Castile to that character. Unamuno probed Spanish history to attempt to rediscover the reasons for the greatness of important figures of the past. He also rediscovered the Castilian landscape and tried to suggest its effect on the inhabitants of this high central plateau. Moreover, he dwelled upon the state of *marasmo* or paralysis which was plaguing the leaders and institutions of Spain around 1898.

Two other early members of the Generation of 98 had a general influence on the poetry of *Fields of Castile*, José Martínez Ruiz (Azorín) and, to a lesser extent, Pío Baroja. As early as 1900, Azorín published *El alma castellana*, followed by the important novels *La voluntad* (1902) and *Antonio Azorín* (1903); the protagonist of the later work established his permanent literary pseudonym. Azorín was especially concerned with the lack of will in modern man, the problem of time, and the Castilian landscape. More concerned with aesthetics in literature than Unamuno, Azorín developed his ability for description of the landscape and of fine detail (of house, room, simple object) until this became his particular forte. He was of poetic temperament, but always wrote prose; in a sense, Machado was lucky in that the writers immediately before him had written prose and left to him the expression of the Castilian theme in verse.

Pío Baroja, especially in his early novels, such as *Camino de perfección* (1903) also explored the Castilian theme with some profundity. Machado, who had met Baroja in Paris, always respected his sincerity, but Baroja rather early revealed a stridency and a nihilistic streak which Machado could not sympathize with.

This discussion of these authors has been kept brief and general, since we can present the details of the Castilian theme adequately by utilizing Machado's poems, but it is only fair to Unamuno and Azorín to stress the fact that they explored the essential aspects of the theme before Machado. He of course brought to the general theme his individuality and his particular experience in Soria.

II *The Castilian Theme*

Our stressing the point that Machado's *Fields of Castile* reveals his contact with the exterior world should not obscure the fact that from the initial poem the poet asserts the individuality of the author of the book, that it is a book of lyric poetry and not an objective historical or sociological study. Being a Spaniard, Machado needed little teaching on the importance of the individual, but certainly in Unamuno he found the theme of the importance of the self, or the uniqueness of each soul, at every turn. Therefore, as the first poem of *Fields of Castile*, Machado proudly placed a "Portrait," a concentrated presentation of both the inward and outward aspects of his experience. The physical details are sketched rapidly: "childhood remembrances of a patio in Seville"; his youth, "twenty years in the land of Castile." The poet recognizes the strong ethical bent of his personality:

> My verse from a serene fountain flows,
> Though in my veins course drops of Jacobin blood;
> And more than a man who well his doctrine knows,
> I am, in the best sense of the word, good.

> *(Hay en mis venas gotas de sangre jacobina,*
> *pero mi verso brota de manantial sereno;*
> *y, más que un hombre al uso que sabe su doctrina,*
> *soy, en el buen sentido de la palabra, bueno.)*

Machado goes on to recognize his early attraction to the aesthetic concerns of Modernism, but scorns the present-day poets whose production is superficial, or "cosmetic." He realizes that, as during the days of *Solitudes*, he is still much alone, but, "Whoever talks to himself hopes to talk with God some day." Finally, the Bohemian days of *Solitudes* are behind him; he is proud to be making his own way. And when the time comes for the ultimate journey, he wants to leave his poetry, "like the captain leaves his sword / Famous for the manly arm that wielded it," and depart, "almost naked, like the sons of the sea."

After the initial "Portrait," *Fields of Castile* continues with a section of poems which explore various facets of the Castilian theme, landscape, and character, ending with a series (which has become widely known) specifically on the landscape around Soria. Machado, who had three opportunities in later editions to arrange the poems, continued to place "On the Banks of the Duero" (XCVIII) in a commanding position; indeed this poem has proved to be Machado's outstanding statement on the Castilian theme in the "bitter" manner. In this manner, common to certain other writers, the Spaniards flagellated themselves by presenting the contrast between the glorious Spain of the Golden Age and her present lowly position after the Spanish-American War, without offering any plan or hope for recovery.

Machado undoubtedly pondered seriously before choosing a form for this poem, and he somewhat surprisingly cast it in Alexandrine couplets. The long and weighty Alexandrine recalls historically the ponderous religious poems of the "four-fold way" of Berceo, one of the medieval poets admired by Machado. More importantly, the *modernistas* such as Darío had recently revived the Alexandrine, though they, supremely conscious of poetry's sound values, concentrated on its sonorous and rhythmical possibilities. The use of the rhyming couplets is even rarer in Machado. Perhaps he was first seized by a couplet, which he continued to turn over in his mind until it became the judiciously repeated refrain of the poem:

> Wretched Castile, triumphant yesterday,
> Wrapped in her rags, she scorns all progress today.

> *(Castilla miserable, ayer dominadora,*
> *Envuelta en sus andrajos desprecia cuanto ignora.)*

Once "committed" to this couplet (as Robert Frost used to say), he perhaps continued his creation of the poem in the same form.

"On the Banks of the Duero" in technique suggests a return to the Romantic manner, in the Wordsworthian sense. At a particular time, a particular place, the poet in solitude makes a physical journey up the hillside toward a place of meditation. The poem begins serenely, with almost forced simplicity: "It was the middle of July. The day was beautiful." (*Mediaba el mes de julio. Era un hermoso día.*)

The poet sets out on his "white road" which borders the Duero and goes down to the Chapel of San Saturio. From here he begins to ascend the small mountain by way of the rock-strewn water courses, and he makes us feel his struggle upward as he leans on his shepherd's staff, conscious of the pungent smell of the mountain plants, rosemary and thyme and sage.

When the poet reaches the summit, he begins to describe the panorama before him, his imagery taking on certain metaphorical qualities. He sees a rounded hill as a "decorated shield," the reddish heights as "Scattered remains of an ancient suit of armor." The river Duero curves around Soria "like the arc of a crossbow," one of Machado's most persistent images. Soria itself is a "defensive bastion toward Aragón." This presentation of the imagery of war introduces one facet of a favorite theme of the Generation of 98, Castile as "warlike and mystic." Obviously Machado is recalling that Soria was a bastion of defense, not only at nearby Numancia in Roman times, but also in the Middle Ages.

As the poet continues to look down upon the river Duero, he

focuses on the Roman bridge crossing it, and under the ancient arches when the waters of the river become "somber," he is overcome by a feeling of melancholy and a series of negative impressions in regard to the Castilian land:

> The Duero crosses the oaken heart of Castile
> And of Iberia. Oh, sad and noble land,
> Land of high plains and desolate rocky heights,
> Of fields without furrows, water or trees;
> Decrepit cities, roads without inns,
> Of dull-eyed rustics, unmoved by dance or song,
> Who go, abandoning a dying home,
> Like your long rivers, Castile, toward the sea!

> *(El Duero cruza el corazón de roble*
> *de Iberia y de Castilla. ¡Oh, tierra triste y noble,*
> *la de los altos llanos y yermos y roquedas*
> *de campos sin arados, regatos ni arboledas;*
> *decrépitas ciudades, caminos sin mesones,*
> *y atónitos palurdos sin danzas ni canciones*
> *que aún van, abandonando el mortecino hogar,*
> *como tus largos ríos, Castilla, hacia la mar!)*

The Duero of course flows through Spain and Portugal into the Atlantic. Here Machado is joining the "outflow" of the rivers and of the people to lament the emigration of the best Castilians to the New World, generally considered an important reason for the impoverishment of Spain.

After this moving passage, the poet interjects his sad and bitter refrain: "Wretched Castile, triumphant yesterday,/ Wrapped in her rags she scorns all progress today." He then proceeds to a negative analysis of Spain, contrasting the present with the past. "Over these fields," he says, "there wanders still the ghost/ Of a people who put God above war." Castile, before the "mother of captains," has become a "stepmother of humble ne'er-do-wells." There is also criticism of the Church, whose leaders have lost their vision: "Philosophers nurtured in the soup of monasteries/ Contemplate impassively the ample firmament." And the poet repeats his refrain.

In a manner typical of the Romantics, the poet comes back to reality at the conclusion. With the sun now setting, he begins his descent toward the town. The simple life of nature goes on as usual as he surprises a pair of "pretty weasels," and the poet makes his way home along the road white with dust. This poem is not particularly long nor are its themes new, but in these concentrated lines Antonio Machado made his first significant step toward becoming known as the poet of the Generation of 98.

The road along the banks of the Duero, which Machado often trod in meditative walks, proved to be the particular place where he meditated upon the essence of Castile and created his poems exploring this theme. He returned to the themes of the previous poem in "Banks of the Duero" (CII). Again he describes the hard and rocky land, the denuded hills, the distant mountains where the eagles dwell; to him this fierce and melancholy land has produced a character, a certain state of consciousness. Again in a stanza he attempts to concentrate the essence of the Castilian people in the land itself:

> Castile of manly virtues, stern land,
> Castile, scorner of Fate's icy breath;
> Castile of pain and ever-present war,
> Immortal land, Castile intimate with death!
>
> *(¡Castile varonil, adusta tierra,*
> *Castilla del desdén contra la suerte,*
> *Castilla del dolor y de la guerra,*
> *Tierra inmortal, Castilla de la muerte!)*

But in this poem, since it is evening, the mood of the poet becomes more lyric as he sees the moon begin to rise; his consciousness is flooded by his customary fusion of dream and time so that the Duero and Castile, and their history in the ballads, become a part of the problem of the eternal:

> And the ancient ballad book,
> Was it some minstrel's dream along your shore?
> O Duero, perhaps like you will Castile be
> In flight down to the sea forevermore?
>
> *(¿Y el viejo romancero*
> *fue el sueño de un juglar junto a tu orilla?*
> *¿Acaso como tú y por siempre, Duero,*
> *irá corriendo hacia la mar Castilla?)*

In a later part of *Fields of Castile*, Machado sought in a few

poems to temper his bitter criticism of Spain in the immediate
past and present by staking his hopes on the younger generation.
His "A Young Spain" (CXLIV) summarizes the political situation at three periods of time, beginning with the Restoration
period of uneasy and deceptive peace before the turn of the
century. Machado, who was then "adolescent," criticizes the
period as a time of "carnival":

> It was a time of lies, of infamy.
> All Spain—drunken, squalid, wretchéd Spain—
> They decked her out in clothes of Carnival
> So that her hands could not explore her wounds.
>
> *(. . . Fue un tiempo de mentira, de infamia. A España toda,*
> *la malherida España, de Carnaval vestida*
> *nos la pusieron, pobre y escuálida y beoda,*
> *para que no acertara la mano con la herida.)*

It was a time of turbulent ideas, premonitions, and deceptions.

Then Machado's own generation appeared, eager to set things
right; Unamuno, Baroja, Azorín, Maeztu, and Machado joined
the skirmish against the system. Yet this generation failed; in a
single biting line, Machado fixes the blame: "But each one the
route of his own madness pursued." Each one tended to retreat
into distant criticism or the creation of his own personal works.[2]
Now, says the poet, writing in 1915, "today is that tomorrow
of yesterday," and still all Spain is dressed in false carnival fin-
ery, with the blood of her wounds now like a "soured wine."
However, the poet insists on a hope in the youth of the younger
generation and their "adventure"; clearly theirs must be a spiritual adventure, springing from a "divine fire,/ Like the diamond
clear, like the diamond pure.

Machado pursues this same theme in "Ephemeral Tomorrow"
(CXXV). His initial criticism of his countrymen is especially bitter. Spain is a place "of brass band and tambourine," all meaningless sound and fury (variations of this "Drum" image were
popular in the period). Spain is also "devoted to Frascuelo and
to María." This juxtapositioning of a popular bullfighter and the
Virgin was jarring to many, and indeed it was unlike Machado.
He goes on to attack a Spain that "prays and yawns." In his dis-
gust, he descends to the revolting imagery of comparing this

spirit which prevails in the country to the nausea of a drunk sick
on soured wine. Yet Machado obstinately dreams of a new
Spain for tomorrow:

> But another Spain is dawning,
> A Spain of artist's chisel and of mace,
> Led by the eternal youth creating itself
> Out of the solid traditions of the race.
> A Spain redemptive and implacable,
> Bursting her ancient cage,
> An avenging hatchet wielded in her hand,
> A Spain of idea and of righteous rage.

> *(Mas otra España nace,*
> *la España del cincel y de la maza,*
> *con esa eterna juventud que se hace*
> *del pasado macizo de la raza.*
> *Una España implacable y redentora,*
> *España que alborea*
> *con un hacha en la mano vengadora,*
> *España de la rabia y de la idea.)*

This is, of course, revolutionary talk. In his ideal moments
Machado envisioned a destruction of the old injustices through
the forces of righteous anger, and the creation of a new order
based on ideas, reason, light. To the end of his life, Machado
clung desperately to these ideas, but hereafter expressed them
in political action during the Civil War.

Machado's penetration of the Castilian environment led him
to a consideration of God as the Castilian type actually conceived Him, especially since, during this period, the poet was
thinking profoundly of the nature of God himself. In "The
Iberian God" (CI), he gives expression to an idea explored by
both him and Unamuno. Machado indicates that the Castilian
peasant, probably from the influence of the Iberian stock, still
retained a concept of a pre-Christian God. The peasant, closely
bound to the land and his crops, retains a god worshipped in
time of plenty and cursed when natural calamities brought time
of famine. But Machado recognizes that the Castilian at one
time also put God in an unassailable position, above war, chance,
earth, and death. At the time, Machado was struggling with the
idea that God is a being each soul helps to create. Therefore he

awaits the appearance of an Iberian "who will carve from the Castilian oak tree/the stern God of the dun-colored land."

While in Soria, Machado was in close contact with the land and people, and again, as was customary with the Romantic poets, he focused on specific elements which evoked in him a strong reaction. A poem of this reaction is "The Poorhouse" (C). The house itself is a ramshackled old dwelling covered with time-blackened tiles, where the black martins nest in summer and around which the ravens croak in winter. Of course the poor inmates are what interest Machado; in the central scene of the poem he presents a still life, suspended in time: at a dirty window, pale and sickly faces with staring eyes look out upon the January day, as snow falls silently on the frigid earth. What is surprising in the poem is its seductive rhythm, achieved with the Alexandrines. These poor characters, which become idiot and criminal types in related poems, awaiting something which is never to come, are of course intended to emphasize the state of degeneracy in Castile.

In the foregoing poems, Antonio Machado generally made clear the amplitude of his theme by the use of words such as "Castile" or "Iberian" even in his titles. Therefore, in order to concentrate on Soria itself, he placed in the heart of *Fields of Castile* a series of nine lyrics entitled "Fields of Soria" (CXIII). The first six of the poems are landscape scenes with peasant figures, suggesting the famous painting by Millet. For example, the fourth is a delicate scene of "The figures of the country against the sky," in which a father drives the oxen while the mother sows the seed. The poet focuses on the child's cradle of reeds carried between the oxen and the "flowing greenish, golden hues / of sunset." While these poems are fine examples of a limited type, it was the last four that became Machado's extremely popular "Soria" poems. What is surprising is that in subsequent editions he failed to reverse the order.

Machado captured forever the essence of Soria for him in these four lyrics. The first begins:

> Soria cold, *Soria pure,*
> *Headland of Extremadura,*
> With its medieval castle
> In ruins, above the Duero;

With its crumbling walls
And houses blackened by time!

(!Soria fría, Soria pura,
cabeza de Extremadura,
con su castillo guerrero
arruinado, sobre el Duero;
con sus murallas roídas
y sus casas denegridas!)

The italicized words are from the town's official crest, which
Machado must have seen first on the old Courthouse in the
heart of Soria. Significantly the poet has added "cold"; in the
Sorian highlands even in July the frigid winds sweep the town,
and in winter the bite of fine snow driven by the blasts was a
memory etched in the poet's consciousness. The reference to
Extremadura is not the southwestern province by that name;
Machado must have read upon an old plaque in chapel San
Saturio the explanation that these "hard extremes" of land were
those upriver and down protected by Soria in the Middle Ages.
The poet goes on in this lyric to chronicle the decadence of the
town; but since he is observing it bathed in moonlight at one
in the morning, it is "beautiful."

In the next lyric the poet begins in a burst of descriptive
eloquence and goes on to seek out the timeless essence of Soria:

Silver-tinted hills,
Gray heights, and rocks of reddish hue,
Where the Duero River makes
Its curving of crossbow's arc
Around Soria. Somber groves of oaks,
Fierce stony ground, the balding mountain peaks,
White roads and river poplars,
Afternoons in Soria, warlike and mystical,
Today I feel for you
In my heart's core a sadness,
Sadness that is love. Sorian fields,
Where even the rocks dream,
You go along with me! Silvered hills,
Gray heights, and rocks of reddish hue!

(¡Colinas plateadas,
grises alcores, cárdenas roquedas
por donde traza el Duero
su curva de ballesta

> *en torna a Soria, oscuros encinares,*
> *ariscos pedregales, calvas sierras,*
> *caminos blancos y álamos del río,*
> *tardes de Soria, mística y guerrera,*
> *hoy siento por vosotros, en el fondo*
> *del corazón, tristeza,*
> *tristeza que es amor! ¡Campos de Soria*
> *donde parece que las rocas sueñan,*
> *conmigo vais! ¡Colinas plateadas,*
> *grises alcores, cárdenas roquedas! . . .)*

Machado's strongest image was of the Duero's curving around
Soria, through the rocky hills, like a crossbow's arc, and he repeated the image over and over with only slight variations. That
the image is military was deliberate: Soria was the bastion of defense for the surrounding region. The gigantic phrase "mystical
and warlike" sums up the Spain of the Golden Age, dominated
by Castile; the phrase evokes such outstanding figures as St.
John of the Cross, Loyola, and the unbelievable *conquistadores*
like Cortés. These fields of Soria therefore evoke in Machado a
sense of history and tradition, while at the same time he humanizes them to the extent that even the rocks have the capacity
to dream.

In the last two lyrics, apparently, the poet is elaborating his
memories. He has returned to his favorite scene to see the poplars along the Duero. These poplars, which sparkle in the sunlight, have carved in their trunks initials of loving couples,
"ciphers that are points in time." Machado at least symbolically
put his initials there, and they thus have become his "word in
time." Therefore these bright poplars (which in dry Castile are
visual symbols of life-giving water) became for Machado a symbol of love. Ultimately the lands of Soria, the deep blue hills,
the roadway by the river, and even the dun-colored earth have
become for the poet a "verdant dream" that has penetrated to
the depths of his soul. His response to the Sorian atmosphere
has been so total and profound that the poet declares that its
qualities were already latent in his soul before he knew Soria.
These Soria poems are another example of Antonio Machado's
ability to evoke an emotional response in us while presenting
the details of his contact with a real world in his moment of
time.

III   La tierra de Alvargonzález
(The Land of Alvargonzález)

In Soria, Antonio Machado, being constantly in quest of the essential Spanish, inevitably turned to the great collections of Spanish ballads, and even reached the conclusion that "the ballad was the supreme expression of poetry."[3] Thus he set out, he tells us in the Prologue to *Fields of Castile*, to write a new Ballad Book, but not in mere imitation of the old one, which was based on heroic deeds. His new ballads were to look toward "the essentially human, the land of Castile, and the book of Moses, called Genesis." Indeed, this last phrase provides the key to the theme of the poem Machado set out to write. In Soria the particular theme which began strongly to interest Machado was the Cain-Abel theme. During this period Unamuno was interested in the same theme (probably before Machado), and produced his novel *Abel Sánchez*. Machado understood this Cain-Abel theme as one of envy and a pre-Christian spirit of vengeance at the heart of the people of Castile. The culmination of this theme in Machado's work became his long narrative poem, *The Land of Alvargonzález*, ultimately included as one of the central poems of *Fields of Castile*.

There is a wealth of detail concerning the writing and publication of *The Land of Alvargonzález*.[4] As Machado came into real contact with the Castilian peasant around Soria (in Madrid he had lived closer to literature), he soon came to believe that the peasant was chiefly interested in tilling the soil and in the occasional violent crimes which occurred. In fact, the number of sensational crimes which took place around 1910 in Soria probably provided an immediate stimulus for his poem. Moreover, certain poems of *Fields of Castile* sketch these themes. In "Around the Lands of Spain" (XCIX), Machado analyzes the peasant, his eyes "always turbid with envy and sadness," a figure who has laid waste his lands "Over which there crosses the errant shadow of Cain." "A Criminal" (CVIII) tells the story of a former seminary student, who, anxious to inherit land from his parents, slays them in a sordid crime and is now awaiting the gallows.

Machado first published *The Land of Alvargonzález* in a prose version. While he was in Paris in 1911, he sold the story to

Rubén Darío, editor of *Mundial* magazine, written in Spanish, and it appeared in January, 1912. Actually the first part of the story has some of Machado's most effective writing. In the first pages he presents the structure of the story: the author has set out to visit the headwaters of the Duero by taking the coach to Cidones (toward Burgos), then continuing on muleback through Covaleda and to the peak of Urbíon, where the river rises. In the tale, a peasant he meets then tells the story of Alvargonzález. The conclusion of the story, however, is abrupt and undeveloped, as if Machado were rushing it to the publisher to pick up a few dollars. It is significant that Machado later chose to forget this version.

The definitive version, in ballad form, appeared in *Fields of Castile* in 1912, just after it had been published in *La Lectura* in Madrid. The ballad tells the tale of an old and prosperous peasant farmer, Alvargonzález, who is murdered and thrown into the Black Lagoon by two of his sons so that they can inherit their father's farm immediately. But they do not prosper. Then the youngest son returns from South America, begins to buy and work the property, and everything prospers. Finally the two murderers, ridden with guilt, are drowned in a mysterious fashion in the same Black Lagoon.

Antonio Machado undoubtedly gave a major effort to the construction of the verses and development of the thematic details in the poem. His was the first effort during his generation to revive the form of the historical ballad with narrative content. He retained the traditional form, with the octosyllable as the basic verse, and with continuing assonance, changed in the vowel combination from section to section. To avoid the monotony caused by end-stopping usual in the old ballads, he occasionally introduces a stop or a pause in the middle of the lines. Machado demonstrates throughout the poem a mastery of the ballad form.

Although in general the details of the poem are realistic, there is an artistic development of various themes and sub-themes. Perhaps the basic one is the theme of the burning hearth, the idea that a perpetually burning fire in the hearth symbolizes the continuity of the home and family. Early in the poem, the older sons cannot light the fire; the fact that the younger can and is thus allowed to by the father, causes the family to be split asunder. In a dream of the father Alvargonzález, his clear preference for the youngest son causes the older sons such envy that they begin to think of patricide:

> The older sons both drift away
> To the corners of their dream.
> Between the pair of fugitives
> An iron hatchet gleams.
>
> *(Los dos mayores se alejan*
> *por los rincones del sueño.*
> *Entre los dos fugitivos*
> *reluce un hacha de hierro.)*

The premonition of the murder, the execution of it by the sons, and subsequent results caused by the murder flow from, and are interwoven with, the theme of the hearth.

After the murder is done, the omens continue, but now they plague the murderers. As they travel along the river, from the Duero's opposite bank they hear a wailing song, which promises that the land of Alvargonzález will produce abundantly again (but not for them); as long as the wrongs are left unsettled, there will be no peace:

> "The land of Alvargonzález once more
> Will teem with things of worth,
> And he who worked the land before
> Sleeps not beneath the earth."
>
> *("La tierra de Alvargonzález*
> *se colmará de riqueza,*
> *y el que la tierra ha labrado*
> *no duerme bajo la tierra.")*

While Miguel, the youngest, prospers, the condition of the older brothers worsens, until even the earth rebels. As one of the brothers attempts to till, "The hoe he sank into the earth / Came out all stained with blood." The brothers finally in desperation return to the Black Lagoon and are themselves mysteriously drowned.

One of the most satisfying elements of the poem is the presentation of the Castilian landscape around Soria. The specific images strong in Machado's consciousness are the same ones he worked and reworked in other poems, so that now many of them are thought of as "Machadian." In a section called "Other Times," "the flowing brambles / and the cherry trees are whitening"; around the towers of the churches the storks are flapping their wings awkwardly; along the riverbank the bright poplars begin to turn green. In the sections of darker mood in the poem there are the "rocky outcroppings" and the high wastelands where the wolves still live. Machado ultimately characterizes the whole region in a single stanza which has become justly famous:

> Oh ancient lands of Alvargonzález
> That lie in the heart of Spain;
> Oh poor and melancholy lands,
> With a soul that feels pain!

> *(!Oh tierras de Alvargonzález*
> *en el corazón de España,*
> *tierras pobres, tierras tristes,*
> *tan tristes que tienen alma!)*

It is clear that for Machado *The Land of Alvargonzález* was intended to be the capstone of his poetry in this period. Thus far the critics have generally accorded it unqualified praise. Of more value is the judgment of José María Valverde, who reasons that Machado had a grand design which was partly unsuccessful, because the poet made "too great a leap and later had to double back."[5] Machado tried to make a significant statement on the whole Spanish problem, and the poem fails partially to make the statement convincingly. Although Valverde does not clearly say why, the reasons go back to the basic concept with which Machado began. The poem sprang, he said, from the Book of Genesis, from an idea of the inextinguishable presence of violent envy or evil in the heart of Man. The poem then becomes a tragedy of Fate, for Alvargonzález is murdered and his sons commit murder without any particular reason or passion; there was no way for the father not to be murdered. Of course, even a modern reader can accept a tragedy of fate, but usually only if the characters involved are authentic. And just here Machado fails: Alvargonzález and his sons are only symbols, or their story is only an allegory, and we never quite suffer with them as characters. Therefore, while Machado was extremely successful in his handling of the octosyllable and in the organization of thematic materials, there remains a shadow of failure over the poem. It is significant that he never again attempted a poem of this magnitude on the Castilian theme in general, though of course the death of his wife and the resulting change of life pattern for him had a bearing on this matter. *The Land of Alvargonzález* sustained the continuing tradition of popular theme and manner in Spanish poetry, the tradition passing from Zorrilla through Machado to Federico García Lorca.

IV   *The Poems of Praise*

During the Castilian period Antonio Machado, in looking outward, pondered seriously upon the task of creating a type of poem at that time generally in disfavor, the *elogio*, or poem of praise. In the Golden Age, Garcilaso, Lope, and Góngora, with the ideal of the Renaissance man strong in their minds, wrote many such poems, usually for the nobility, but the type had gradually been appropriated by second-rate poets writing poor poems in praise of personal friends. Machado sought to revive the type with a double aim: the recognition and encouragement of "select spirits," usually men of letters rather than nobles as before, and the addition of his own poetic themes. In a letter to Juan Ramón Jiménez in 1912, he discusses his project: "I try to place myself initially in the point of view of some select spirits and to continue in myself those various impulses in a common channel, toward an ideal outlook." Only in the joint effort of the select spirits can the future be assured, for as the poet emphasizes: "If we do not form a single vital and impetuous current, Spanish inertia will triumph."[6] As we have seen, Machado was always of generous spirit, and capable of recognizing excellence in a person with whom he disagreed on basic issues.

It is fitting that we begin with "To Don Miguel de Unamuno" (CLI), for indeed this great Basque figure was the first of his generation to call for men of great moral and spiritual stature. His motto became "Inward"; only in self-searching could a man create himself. For Machado, "This donquixotic / Don Miguel de Unamuno, mighty Basque, / Wears the grotesque harness . . . / Of the good Manchegan." Thus like Don Quixote, to a people of muledrivers, gamblers, and such, he preaches lessons of chivalry. Above all, Machado emphasizes in the concluding lines Unamuno's sanctity and sincerity: "And he is as good or better than Loyola; / He smacks of Jesus, spits on the Pharisee." (*Y es tan bueno y mejor que fue Loyola;/ sabe a Jesús y escupe al fariseo.*) Later Machado dedicated another poem (CLXII) "To the Iberian giant Miguel de Unamuno, through whom present-day Spain is achieving honor in the world."

Of all the poems of the *elogio* type, perhaps the best as a poem is one (CXVII) of the two Machado wrote for Azorín on the publication of the latter's *Castile*. With this book, Azorín consolidated his reputation as the poet-in-prose of the Castilian landscape. Machado was perhaps closer in spirit to Azorín (especially during this period) than he was to his own brother Manuel, and his many dedications to Azorín indicate his awareness of it. Machado's poem, written in fine Alexandrine couplets, has its locale in his own part of northern Castile: "The inn of Cidones stands near the main road / Between Soria and Burgos." The poet goes on in realistic fashion to create a homelike scene in the inn: The innkeeper (a typical Castilian peasant type) stares into the fireplace, where his wife watches supper boiling in a kettle. Seated at a pine table, writing, is a "gentleman," lost in thought, who is suspiciously like Azorín. While the gentleman is awaiting the mail coach, he too contemplates the flame and the flickering shadows, and is finally overcome by the power of his memories. The arrival of the mail coach brings him back to the present. This short poem is an outstanding example of Antonio Machado's ability to create a scene of simple intimacy in an objective setting.

One of the figures greatly respected by Machado and all his generation was Don Francisco de Giner, not a literary man but an educator. Although he apparently taught Antonio as a boy at the Free Institute, he was of another generation and Machado undoubtedly never knew him intimately. When he died in 1915, Machado wrote and read in public his tribute to the man who through work and education hoped for a better Spain (XXXIX):

... Observe for me
A mourning period of labor and of hope.
Be good, no more; be what I have been
Among you: spirit.
Live, for life goes on,
The dead die and all the shadows pass . . .
Ring out, anvils; let all the bells be mute!

(. . . hacedme
un duelo de labores y esperanzas,
Sed buenos y no más, sed lo que he sido
entre vosotros: alma.
Vivid, la vida sigue,
los muertos mueren y las sombras pasan; . . .
¡Yunques, sonad; enmudeced, campanas!)

Then the poet urges his friends to carry the body to "the blue hills of the wide Guadarrama Mountains," and there to bury him under one of the "chaste oaks." For Machado in Madrid, the Guadarrama Mountains, which rise to the north of the city, were a natural symbol of elevation; the small *encina* oak was his symbol of Castilian fortitude.

Machado also admired the brilliant young philosopher José Ortega y Gasset, although he disagreed basically with some of Ortega's early positions on questions concerning Spain. Ortega completed his education in Germany and became a great admirer of German scholarship and methods; therefore as a young man he began to agitate for a complete Europeanization of Spain. At one point he was ready to disown the Catholic literary heritage of Spain, except for the *Quixote.* (Unamuno at one period was guilty of the same rejection; some even called him a great "Protestant.") Machado admired in Ortega his profound scholarship, his interest in rebuilding Spain along European lines, and his brilliance as a writer. The exceptional form of Machado's *elogio,* of staccato, intellectualized lines in a very brief lyric, indicates that Ortega is an exceptional subject:

With laurel and ivy
Be crowned, favorite
of Sophia, architect.

(A ti laurel y yedra
corónente, dilecto
de Sofía, arquitecto.)

Clearly Ortega is thought of as a builder, an "architect," of "another somber Escorial." Inevitably Machado links Ortega with the builder of the original Escorial, the Emperor Philip II:

> And may austere Philip . . .
> From the edge of his regal sepulcher,
> Look out to see the new architecture,
> And bless the offspring of Luther.
>
> *(Y que Felipe austero . . .*
> *al borde de su regia sepultura,*
> *asome a ver la nueva arquitectura,*
> *y bendiga la prole de Lutero.)* (CXL)

Machado does not reject Ortega's introduction of "Protestant" culture into a rigidly Catholic country insofar as this culture implies intellectual progress, but the tone of the poem suggests his wonderment at possible results.

The section of *"Elogios"* contains other poems of value. There are two for the poet Rubén Darío, a strong influence on Machado's early years. There are two for his brother poet Juan Ramón Jiménez, whose later poetic manner Machado questioned, though his admiration for the poet never wavered. There is one for Xavier Valcarce, a friend of Machado's, today known only through this *elogio*. Finally there is one for the medieval religious poet Gonzalo de Berceo, whose simple monotonous lines and ingenuous religious outlook touched a responsive chord in the complex Machado. That Machado was successful with his *elogios* is proved by the fact that scholars have repeatedly utilized his penetrating lines in their studies of the figures he praised.

V *The Memory of Human Love*

In the organization of his *Fields of Castile*, Antonio Machado in subsequent editions continued to place a number of poems relating to his love for Leonor, principally in *Morte,* after *The Land of Alvargonzález*. Although the poems do not quite blend into the book, certainly Machado considers them expressions of his "looking outward," of his human contact with the people as well as the land. His love for Leonor was an essential aspect of his "five years in Castile," and he preserved and explored the memory of that love far beyond the Castilian period. We have already described the dangerous shock of Leonor's premature death upon him, and his first poems reflect that shock. Later, with his usual honesty, the poet suffered the agony of seeing fade what he had thought would be a permanent memory.

Of the beginnings, the growth and the fullness of his love for Leonor, Antonio Machado left us only silence, and indeed there is only one lyric of value before her death. Machado was a reticent man; like most of his generation he had a horror of displaying the intimacy of his love for a woman. One playful little lyric has survived his somewhat difficult courtship. It was not lost upon the grave and scholarly Antonio, beyond thirty, that Leonor was almost a child. Therefore he fears that the lass he loves will prefer "a sprightly young barber." His first serious poem relating to Leonor is "To a Withered Elm" (CXV), which almost passes as a nature poem. Machado, however, took care to date it in the spring of 1912, when he returned to Soria with Leonor in badly failing health. The poet begins by describing "The centenary elm upon the hill / Bathed by the Duero." The lightning-blasted old tree is half rotten, its decaying trunk eaten by ants. But what interests the poet is that with the coming of spring the aging tree has bravely put forth a few green leaves. With Leonor now in the last desperate months of her life, Machado in his final lines pleads for a miracle for her:

> My heart also stands
> In wait, toward light and toward life
> Another miracle of the coming spring.

> *(Mi corazón espera*
> *también, hacia la luz y hacia la vida,*
> *otro milagro de la primavera.)*

But the miracle was not to come, and not long after he buried her in the Espino cemetery and fled Soria, he compressed into a single quatrain of rhymed Alexandrines the bitter reality of his being driven again into solitude (CXIX):

> Lord, Thou hast snatched away that which I held most dear.
> Hear, once again, my God, my heart cry out to Thee.

Thy will was carried out, O Lord, against my own.
Lord, we are all alone, my heart and the sea.

(Señor, ya me arrancaste lo que yo más quería.
Oye otra vez, Dios mío, mi corazón clamar.
Tu voluntad se hizo, Señor, contra la mía.
Señor, ya estamos solos mi corazón y el mar.)

Three tender poems follow (CXV ff), in which the poet, finding refuge again "in dreams," struggles to retain the hope always a part of his consciousness. "Beat on, heart, not everything / Has earth swallowed up" ends one; and another: "Live on, hope, who knows / What earth will swallow up!"

During the first spring after Leonor's death, Machado, now living in the dry and warmer region of Baeza in Andalucía, collects his memories of her and spring and Soria and succeeds in composing one of his most remembered poems (CXXV).[7] The poet utilizes the epistolary manner as a structure, a form introduced into Spanish literature by Boscán and Garcilaso during the Renaissance. In late April of 1913, Machado writes to a literary and personal friend, José María Palacio, editor of a Sorian journal. The poet wonders if spring has finally reached the high land of Soria:

Palacio, dear friend, is Spring
Now decking out the branches of the poplars
Along the river and the country roads?
In the highlands of the Duero spring comes late,
But when it comes it is so beautiful and sweet!
Have the ancient elms put out
Those first tender leaves?
The acacia trees will still be standing bare,
And capped with snow the peaks along the range.
Oh, rounded crest of Moncayo, pink and white,
Far off against the skies of Aragón, how fair!

(Palacio, buen amigo,
¿está la primavera
vistiendo ya las ramas de los chopos
del río y los caminos? En la estepa
del alto Duero, primavera tarda,
¡pero es tan bella y dulce cuando llega! . . .
¿Tienen los viejos olmos
algunas hojas nuevas?

Aún las acacias estarán desnudas
y nevados los montes de las sierras.
¡Oh, mole del Moncavo blanco y rosa,
allá, en el cielo de Aragón, tan bella!)

With care the poet evokes in his memory the remembered image of nature: the white-flowering brambles, the white daisies in the fine grasses, the cherry tree in bloom, and of course his harbingers of spring, the storks fluttering awkwardly around the belltower. Thus far the poet has given us a nature poem, extolling the sweetness of spring. Obviously now Machado has mastered the wild emotion he felt when he reacted to Leonor's death; he is returning to a sense of resignation and control that was always a part of his character. Without changing tone, he introduces the specific message of the letter:

. . . Palacio, dear friend,
Are the nightingales now back along the shore?
With the lilies first in bloom
And first-blooming roses from the garden near,
One azure evening go up to the Espino,
The high Espino graveyard where her land is . . .

(. . . Palacio, buen amigo,
¿tienen ya ruiseñores las riberas?
Con los primeros lirios
y las primeras rosas de las huertas,
en una tarde azul, sube al Espino,
al alto Espino donde está su tierra . . .)

Palacio's mission to "go up to the high Espino" is both a fact and a symbol, for the cemetery stands on a hill with its own church, in whose shadow Leonor lies buried.

This is a simple poem, but a fine example of what Antonio Machado called his "word in time" (*palabra en el tiempo*). It makes eternal a particular moment, touched and transformed by the power of memory, of a particular man in a particular place, living his human existence. Machado feared, in what has come to be called the Existentialist philosophy, that this was all he had, and he strove honorably to make the best of it.

As the years passed, Machado felt his memory of the loved one fading, and the inevitable resurgence of a desire in his spirit to look outward again. His poem "Parergon," the Greek word for "Leavings," explores this new state of mind. Subtitled "Eyes," we should suspect a poem in his metaphysical manner, for the eyes become for him a symbol of the "essential heterogeneity of being." In this poem, however, which seems to be a complex structure of three parts, the poet is actually exploring the complexities of memory. In the first part the poet tells us that when his loved one died he sought to "close his mansion," make time stop, keep his memories intact: "All a yesterday in the clear mirror." But a year or so later, he finds to his horror that he cannot remember even the color of her eyes—sea-green, gray, black? In the last part, he goes out on the street again, sees a girl looking at him from a window, and his memory is shockingly revived. The eyes were like those of the beloved! Thus his love and the memory of it become a changing process, leading him on to another experience, in spite of his hesitancy.

In 1922, the poet was still tied to his memories, but he was beginning to change. The intimacy of his past experiences was gone; he indicates this by turning to the demanding form of the sonnet, with its more formalized expression. In the first two of a series of four sonnets (CLXIV), he calls upon his "obedient remembrance" and it obeys dutifully by giving him his old images of nature in Soria. The final image in the sequence is of the graveyard in Soria: "The whitewashed wall, the pointed cypress trees." The third sonnet is formal in the Renaissance manner with powerful but generalized images. The fourth and last begins by stressing his solitude, but there appears "a lady with a veiled face," and the poet is attracted by the "mystery of her loving voice." The poet is slowly finding his way back into the world.

By 1924, Machado knew that his remembrance of Leonor had faded, that her place in his emotional experiences was becoming consecrated. He published another series of four sonnets (CLXV), but only one of them concerns Leonor. Significantly, the first phrase of this sonnet emphasizes the intense ethical preoccupations constant in the mature Machado: "Have I besmirched your memory? How many times?" As he was to confess in *Juan de Mairena*, he had never been able to escape from "that labyrinth of good and evil, not even in dreams." A sense of duty, a constancy in conduct were of course aspects of that moral sense. The sonnet goes on to contrast two of his important symbols, the river and the fountain. Here the river suggests life as inevitable change, in the Heraclitan sense; the fountain is concerned with a clearer essence of a more eternal nature. Therefore, he has preserved the sublimated essence of this simple human love in the fountain of his inner consciousness: "And there your name resounds—eternally!" The memory of Leonor thus remained as a soft glow of piety, much like the moral force Laura exerted upon an older Petrarch.

VI   *Conclusion*

In the latter part of *Fields of Castile* stands a long poem unique in tone and manner in Machado's verse. Called "Poem for a Day" (CXXVIII) and subtitled "Rural Meditations," this poem in a sense marks the beginning of the end of his poetic venture of looking outward, for in it the poet with minute detail and a matter-of-fact tone discusses his abject loneliness and his retreat again into the philosophical. Although we would expect blank verse or a free form in this prosy situation, actually the poet employs a variation of the form used by Jorge Manrique in his famous medieval elegy. Machado utilizes this tightly-rhyming form (and even adds rhyming couplets) to effect a certain ironic humor, as we see in the opening lines:

> Behold me now, professor
> Of modern tongues (yesterday
> Apprentice of the nightingale
> And master of the festive lay . . .)

> *[Heme aquí ya, professor*
> *de lenguas vivas (ayer*
> *maestro de gay-saber,*
> *aprendiz de ruiseñor . . .)]*

Although there is a strong sense of solitude in this meditative poem, the poet is keenly aware of his surroundings. Outside a heavy mist is falling, at times rain, at times snow, and in this heavy atmosphere the poet becomes conscious of the insistent ticking of the clock. This leads him to ponder upon the meaning of time. The falling raindrops then catch his attention, and his thoughts follow a progression from the drops of water to the fountain, to the river, and down to the sea. The contemplation of this symbol of the sea evokes the "reason and madness and bitterness" of desperately wanting to believe and not being able to.

The poet turns from this disturbing thought to his book-shelves, where as usual there is a jumble of old and new books and papers. Not surprisingly, his eye alights upon Unamuno's latest book, never named, but which must be *The Tragic Sense of Life*. As always, its philosophy is "water from the blessed spring," that is, essential comment upon life. Machado, as an "humble professor of a rural Institute," again declares his loyalty to Unamuno and his ideas.

Then his eyes fall upon what must be a well-thumbed volume of Henri Bergson, *Les données immédiates de la conscience*. Since we know that he had been strongly impressed by Bergson's lectures in Paris, his reaction is surprising: "This Bergson is a cunning rogue; / Right, Maestro Unamuno?" (*Este Bergson es un tuno; / ¿Verdad, maestro Unamuno?*)

As Machado goes on to explain, he is focusing on one of the lesser-emphasized aspects of Bergson's philosophy. The book of Bergson just mentioned has been translated into English as *Time and Free Will*, an indication of its content. While permanently influenced by Bergson's ideas on being and intuition, Machado is here commenting upon the idea of free will: "This devilish Jew / Has found free will / Right in his own skull." What Machado is saying in jest, Bergson of course expounded seriously. Whereas in earlier periods, such as the Renaissance, the arguments over free will and predestination reached something of a standoff, Bergson, utilizing his definitions of time and being, argued that each individual must have free will, whether he wants it or not. Machado ironically accepts this sobering idea by declaring:

Not bad:
To each wise man his problem,
To each madman his theme.

> *(No está mal:*
> *cada sabio, su problema,*
> *y cada loco, su tema.)*

These thorny philosophical problems keep going round and round in his head until he reaches the ultimate impasse: "Solitude of solitudes, / Vanity of vanities." With this, as Antonio Machado had done and was to do all his life, he grabs his hat and "takes to the road." Although he knows what he will find in the streets of provincial Baeza, he goes outside for the reassuring contact with other people, and the banalities and monotonies of life. Just as he expects, the conversation of the small-town characters is predictable: Don Juan wonders why the liberals are moral reprobates, Don José argues that the conservatives work no wonders, and both agree that everything changes sooner or later. "That's life," both of the old gentlemen pontificate; then their talk drifts easily to the blessings of the rain, the growth of the crops, and the fact that God usually sends the rain at the proper time.

His outlook made serener by the familiar monotony of the lives of his fellow human beings, the poet has returned to his room in the last scene of the poem. Bergson's *Time and Free Will* still lies upon the table, but in his inner being he is now ready to face solitude again:

> Things are all right
> With the fundamental "I,"
> Contingent and free, at times
> Creative and original . . .

> *(No está mal*
> *este yo fundamental,*
> *contingente y libre, a ratos,*
> *creativo, original . . .)*

However, he retains a skeptical attitude toward the power of the "I," Bergson's consciousness; for him consciousness still resides in "this mortal flesh" and is seeking to reach beyond itself, toward what he later called "otherness," the ultimate otherness of course being God.

Despite a certain raggedness of structure traceable to the inclusion of poems of somewhat diverse theme and manner (such as the one just discussed), *Fields of Castile* is a solid human document of a type more and more difficult for modern poets to write. It is his effort to look outward toward the real world, toward the Spanish cultural and political problems, and the Castilian landscape, toward the colleagues pursuing the same enterprise, and toward the creation of a personal life. At the same time, it is interesting how this book emphasizes a continuity with *Solitudes*. For example, the symbolic "river" of *Solitudes* he actually discovered in the Duero in Soria, and the symbolic "white road" of *Solitudes* he actually found, winding along the river. Moreover, his preoccupation with temporality is reexpressed in the strong sense of history in Soria as a typical town of Castile. He even humanizes the landscape of Soria until the very rocks are dreaming. When his wife's tragic death aborted his experience in looking outward, the presence of Soria became more vivid in his process of memory. *Fields of Castile* can be meaningfully compared to Robert Frost's books of New England theme. Both poets, originally from other places, found in their new locations of Castile and New England a world adequate for poetry with symbolic overtones. Both Frost and Machado created a type of poetry now become a bit old-fashioned, but with a quality we moderns are likely to envy rather than scorn.

CHAPTER 4

The Poet as Metaphysician

T HE third and final period in Antonio Machado's poetic production is complex, difficult, and shot through with paradoxes, but ultimately rewarding to the reader as the culmination of his poetic career. Very early Machado had felt himself wavering between poetry and philosophy, between intuition and conceptual knowledge. *Solitudes* ends in a retreat into the philosophical; the period of *Fields of Castile* also tends to dribble away into philosophical and social concerns. Essentially, the poet's aesthetic preoccupations came under the pressure of his ethical and even didactic concerns. By 1925, moreover, Machado was feeling the real pressure of the new generation of poets, a pressure which forced him to strive for a renovation of his own poetry. In his renovation, therefore, it was natural that he attempt to blend together the metaphysical and the poetic. As he summarized it, "Every poet . . . supposes a metaphysics; perhaps each poem ought to have its own—implicit, of course, never explicit—and the poet has the duty of expounding it, separately, in clear concepts."[1] Ultimately he reached an even stronger conclusion: "Some day poets and philosophers will exchange roles. The poets will sing of their astonishment in the presence of the great metaphysical deeds; the philosophers will speak to us of anguish, the essentially poetic anguish of being close to nothingness . . ."[2]

Machado's attempts to blend the philosophical and the poetic begins in a rather simple way. For a number of years he devoted considerable effort to a long series of "Proverbs and Songs," one-stanza poems which usually present a grain of philosophy in tightly concentrated poetic form. The first series, which appeared in *Fields of Castile*, was written during the years 1909-17; the second, published in *New Songs*, was composed in 1923-24. His later system of "poet's metaphysics" is a continued development of ideas from these "Proverbs."

But the major poems of the third period and the "metaphysical support" in prose for their creation appear in a complex section of the *Complete Works* called finally the *Cancionero apócrifo* (*Apocryphal Songbook*), itself in two parts, the poems and prose of which were published at different dates, from 1926 to 1933. This book is intimately connected with the crisis in his life and work around 1926, involving his autumn love for Guiomar and a rebirth of his artistic energies. Just as he turned to drama so as to represent himself in the protagonists of his plays, in his *Apocryphal Songbook* he created a series of *personae* through which to project himself. In the first of the two parts, the *persona* is Abel Martín, poet and philosopher, who supposedly lived from 1840 to 1898. In the second he adds Juan de Mairena, also a figure of the past (1856-1909), who was a student and biographer of Martín. Machado creates also a third *persona* of brief appearance, Jorge Meneses, whose initials indicate that he springs from Mairena, not from Machado directly.[3]

Machado's reasons for creating this profusion of *personae* are fairly clear. He showed reluctance when it came to presenting philosophy under his own name, since he lacked systematic training in this discipline. Moreover, the poems express the three great themes of Love, God, and Death, and in all cases he felt a need for distance. The love poems were for him disturbingly intimate; his concept of God was shocking in Catholic Spain; and for the poems on death, he preferred to project the death of his *persona* Abel Martín. Of central importance is the fact that the whole book is saturated with an anguished ironic humor which our discussion will attempt to explore.

I   The "Proverbs and Songs"

Machado's extensive collection of "Proverbs and Songs" traces in a clear and forceful manner the growth of his skepticism, and to them he devoted many hours of vigil. Their double title suggests the two sources from which they spring. In one of them Machado himself suggests a distant source for his proverbs:

> Like don Sem Tob of old,
> We tint our graying locks,
> With more reason than he.

(Como don Sem Tob,
se tiñe las canas
y con más razón.)

That is, modern man must use any desperate means to prolong his brief temporal existence. This Rabbi Sem Tob, an obscure figure of the fourteenth century, left a book of *Moral Proverbs*, pithy stanzas (much like Machado's) of common wisdom. A critic has made a meaningful comparison of some of his "Proverbs" with Sem Tob's,[4] but Machado's debt was undoubtedly quite general. Because of the great gulf in time and outlook between them, Machado surely evoked the old Rabbi's name as another touch of humor.

Machado was also from early days fascinated by the distilled wisdom in poetic form of the Andalusian *cantares*. Although the poet often utilized the *copla* form (usually a stanza of three or four lines, with assonance), the substance of his "Proverbs and Songs" lacks traditional *copla* material; as popular poetry, this usually expresses some variation of the theme of love. In a very few examples, tinged with ironic humor, Machado evokes the Andalusian character:

A gypsy conversation:
"How are things, old friend?"
"Round and round in the shortcut."

(Conversación de gitanos:
−¿Cómo vamos, compadrito?
−Dando vueltas al atajo.)

The substance of most of Machado's "Proverbs and Songs" concerns his growing skepticism. In the group of fifty-three which he reprinted in *Fields of Castile*,[5] this skepticism is based on his acceptance of the ancient conclusion of Ecclesiastes on the vanity of all things. From the beginning, however, he makes it clear that his struggle is not with his fellow man but with God, with the ultimate philosophical problems. Indeed, he forcefully expresses what was always his human position:

Think it not strange, sweet friends,
That my brow is creased with ruts;
I live at peace with fellow men,
My war burns in my guts.

(No extrañeís, dulces amigos,
que esté mi frente arrugada;
yo vivo en paz con los hombres
y en guerra con mis entrañas.)

While he often attacks the malice and stupidity of mankind in general, he continually invites the individual to participate with him in the pursuit of truth.

In the "Proverbs" Machado evokes the name of Jesus, a figure of great attraction for him, but his idea of Jesus is never orthodox. He insists in preserving the "divinity" of Jesus; however, his Jesus is a man who "made" or created his own divinity. It is significant that when he utilizes one of Jesus' most stunning miracles, he twists it so that he is emphasizing, not the miracle, but his own skepticism:

> And why do we call roads
> The furrows of destiny?
> For all who journey walk,
> Like Jesus, upon the sea.
>
> *(¿Para qué llamar caminos*
> *a los surcos del azar? . . .*
> *Todo el que camina anda,*
> *como Jesús, sobre el mar.)*

This idea that each soul is caught up in the irreversible flow of time, each one in its own unique isolation, and that there is no "way," is reaffirmed in one of his longer and most famous proverbs:

> Wayfarer, your footprints are
> The road, and nothing more;
> There is no road, wayfarer,
> By walking we make the road.
> We make the road by walking,
> And when we look behind
> We see the path that none
> Will ever tread again.
> Wayfarer, there is no road,
> Just wakes upon the sea.
>
> *(Caminante, son tus huellas*
> *el camino, y nada más;*
> *caminante, no hay camino,*
> *se hace camino al andar.*

> *Al andar se hace camino,*
> *y al volver la vista atrás*
> *se ve la senda que nunca*
> *se ha de volver a pisar.*
> *Caminante, no hay camino,*
> *sino estelas en la mar.)*

If Machado's Jesus is a figure more human than divine, it is with God Himself that his most desperate struggles take place. Machado strives like the mystics, but in a much more desperate plight. Their struggle was in reaching a God they firmly believed to exist; Machado's problem is that he believes he must almost create God himself for Him to exist. Man has two battles, says Machado: awake he struggles with the "sea," which is death; in "dreams" he struggles with God. And in the anguished skepticism of these proverbs, his worsening illusion reaches desperation. He very effectively uses the dream motif, but in a manner more intense than before:

> Yesterday I dreamed of seeing God,
> Toward Him my words were streaming;
> I even dreamed He heard my voice,
> I later dreamed I was dreaming.

> *(Ayer soñé que veía*
> *a Dios y que a Dios hablaba;*
> *y soñé que Dios me oía . . .*
> *Después soñé que soñaba.)*

To dream he is dreaming is obviously not one but two steps removed from reality. In another proverb he even inverts the situation of the dreaming-waking motif:

> Last night I dreamed of hearing God,
> Whose voice was shouting: "Hearken!"
> I later dreamed that God was sleeping,
> And I was shouting: "Awaken!"

> *(Anoche soñé que oía*
> *a Dios, gritandome: ¡Alerta!*
> *Luego era Dios quien dormía,*
> *y yo gritaba: ¡Despierta!)*

If the poet is not creating God, at least his active participation is essential if a vital relationship is to exist between God and himself. In these two related proverbs, Machado, utilizing one of his favorite themes, achieves an intensity and a concentration both philosophical and poetic at the same time.

In the second long series of ninety-nine "Proverbs and Songs," published in *New Songs*,[6] there is not an essential change of manner, only a shift of emphasis. His desperate reaching out toward God almost disappears. Apparently Machado was conscious of not wanting to repeat himself, as this proverb perhaps indicates:

> A single symbol abides:
> *Quod elixum est ne asato.*
> Don't roast what's already fried.

> *(Sólo quede un símbolo:*
> quod elixum est ne asato.
> *No aséis lo que está cocido.)*

At the same time, the ironic humor is becoming intensified. Above all, the poet begins to assume more contact with the world about him.

Around 1924, with a new generation pushing him, Machado feels the pressure for renovation in his work. As he puts it succinctly:

> *O rinnovarsi o perire ...*
> Does not sound good to me.
> *Navigare è necessario ...*
> Live in order to see.

> *(*O rinnovarsi o perire ...
> *No me suena bien.*
> Navigare è necessario ...
> *Mejor: ¡vivir para ver!)*

To renovate or perish faces every aging poet, but Machado is suggesting that first he must again "live" his experience in time; then he can "see" properly—for him "seeing" is seeing things poetically. In these proverbs there is veiled evidence of a personal kind that the poet is enjoying a renewal of vitality. Once, he says, he stirred the cold ashes of his hearth—and burned his hand. Among proverbs of more abstract manner, he slips this one, which must apply to him personally:

Is the new sap running riot?
Little tree, take care
That no one find it out.

(¿Ya sientes la savia nueva?
Cuida, arbolillo,
que nadie lo sepa.)

And the poet finally asserts his conclusion definitively: "Lend me your ears: / A heart in solitude / Is not a heart."

In the second series of "Proverbs and Songs," Machado attempts to develop this intuition of a basic duality in life into a philosophy. The series finished, he placed this philosophical proverb in the commanding first position:

The eye you see is not an eye
So that you may it see;
It's an eye, for it sees you.

(El ojo que ves no es
ojo porque tú lo veas;
es ojo porque te ve.)

This eye becomes his essential symbol for consciousness or being. What he is doing here first is denying the subjectivism so important to him before. This proverb, which he repeats with at least ten variations, becomes the metaphysical base for his idea of "the essential heterogeneity of being." From it he is to develop his poetry on love, God, and death in his last period. Since the prose of the *Apocryphal Songbook* develops the idea of this proverb, we shall return to it in the coming section. Along with this proverb, we must place a stunning one of a single, intensely concentrated octosyllable, perhaps his most essential line: "Today is always yet" (*Hoy es siempre todavía*). This is his octosyllable of temporality. The today-always-yet sweeps time present, past, and future; and above all, the "yet" tells him that although he is aging, time is still "pregnant with imminences," still rich in possibilities for poetic creation.

II   *The Metaphysics of the* Apocryphal Songbook

To put the poetry and prose of the *Apocryphal Songbook* in the perspective Machado intended, it is a necessary (but almost impossible) task to try to present in a few pages the thorny metaphysics it contains.[7] Machado proceeds in haphazard fashion, sometimes retreating into humor at points of difficulty; indeed, he confesses that his discussion is a "poet's metaphysics," at times obscure. At the beginning, reporting the ideas of Abel Martín, he commences in serious fashion by indicating that his point of departure is found in the philosophy of Leibnitz. Like Leibnitz, he conceives of substance as something constantly active, as energy or force which can engender movement and is always its cause, but which also subsists without movement. The activity of substance is called consciousness. This conscious activity, through which substance is revealed, is characterized by perpetual change. At this point Martín (now following Bergson) is careful to distinguish between movement and mutability. Mere movement supposes a change of position of objects in space. On the contrary, mutability, or change of substance, cannot be thought conceptually; it must be intuited by consciousness itself, which Martín also calls being.

Martín departs from Leibnitz' philosophy at an essential point. Leibnitz conceived of substance as a plurality of monads, or individual souls, each one in communication only with God. Martín rejects the idea of a plurality of monads; for him there is only a single monad of active consciousness which is the universe itself. Martín projects this monad in an expansive, Oriental-sounding metaphor as *the great eye which sees all on seeing itself.* While this metaphor seems to suggest a pantheistic God embracing all, it is of great importance that Martín rejects the idea of the soul's communication with God. In fact, Martín's God is completely unorthodox, as we shall see in a moment. Martín progresses toward his idea of "the essential heterogeneity of being," by which he is emphasizing the almost absolute isolation of his consciousness, or his own soul.

Early in his career, he jotted down in moments of intuition some Andalusian *coplas*, from which "by reflection and analysis he drew all his metaphysics." In his first *copla*, he rejects subjectivism. In his second, he plunges toward otherness: "Thanks, Petenera mine; / In your eyes I lost myself; / It was just what I wished." In a third *copla*, he concludes sardonically: "Without woman / There is neither begetting nor knowledge."

It soon becomes obvious that Martín is really interested in the problem of love between man and woman. Having just declared that the universe (that his universe) is a single active monad, he is nevertheless disturbed by the "four appearances," namely movement, the extension of matter, cognitive limitations, and the multiplicity of subjects. This latter appearance, the multiplicity of subjects, for Abel Martín the poet involves the "passion-invoking problem of love." The aging Martín has always been an "extremely erotic" man, he confesses, and his woman-centered *coplas* certainly prove the point. In his first book, *The Five Forms of Objectivity*, Martín dismisses four forms, saying they are actually subjective, among them even the world of science. What interests Martín is the fifth form, which he ironically confesses has only a *pretension* of being objective, but he insists that somewhere at the outer limits of his own consciousness, he has discovered "a real *otherness*, an object not of knowledge, but of love." Martín supposedly exhausted this idea in his second long book, *From the One to the Other*.

Martín develops his idea of love by presenting four sonnets, each followed by further metaphysical discussion. Love begins to reveal itself as a sudden upsurge in the stream of life, the love object not yet having appeared at all. In his first sonnet, "Springtime," Martín feels a "double throbbing": his heart shouts at him and his thought deafens him. Thus both heart and head (and by extension poet and philosopher) search for the feminine "Thou." Therefore, Martín declares with a new twist, the beloved is one with the lover, not at the end of the process, but at the beginning. This is admittedly a rejection of the mystics; for Martín, both monks and nuns, in their playing with erotic imagery, were "as disturbed as they were ignorant." Martín proceeds to develop further his idea of love in a negative manner. Love does not begin, as in Plato, in the contemplation of the beautiful figure of woman or of the beautiful lad, thence to be sublimated toward ideal beauty. For Martín the incentive of love is not beauty; it is the "metaphysical thirst for the essentially other." And since this thirst is metaphysical, slaking it becomes an impossibility. In his poetic way Martín declares, "The beloved does not keep the date"; love itself is "a sense of absence."

In spite of the chilling suggestion of these words, Martín proceeds with his fourth sonnet, through which his distant creator Machado reveals the secret toward which he has been heading:

Nel mezzo del camin there pierced my breast
The Cupid's arrow of an untimely love . . .

*(*Nel mezzo del camin *pasomé el pecho*
la flecha de un amor imtempestivo . . .)

Untimely it was, but this love shook the aging poet to the depths
of his being and evoked a concentrated flood of poetry. But he
goes on to doom himself in this very sonnet. "If a grain of
thought could burn, / Not in the lover, but in love itself, it
would be / The deepest thought ever seen," he says. Yet he has
already declared ironically that the lover cannot get outside himself, that all objectivity is really only appearance. His later conclusion is that, "in lyrical terms, the beloved is impossible." In
fact, his idea of love has convinced him of "the essential heterogeneity of being," a favorite phrase and the title of another of
Martín's books. For Martín, love offers one premium; in his
"intrasubjective metaphysics," the "reward of love is knowledge." This "knowledge" means that the poet understands the
abject human condition of isolation within the self, and that his
only recourse is manfully to sing his vital, unique experience.

At this point, apparently wearying of his tortured metaphysics, Martín gives us a series of "vaguely related" poems, "Coun-
sels, *Coplas*, Notes." These thirteen tiny poems, in fact, trace
the poet Machado's whole emotional history to the present.
There is a suggestion of a childhood memory, of his wife, of his
period of abstract songs. He rapidly reaches the agonizing
period of his autumn love for Guiomar:

Upon the sea of woman
Few shipwreck at night;
Many at morning's light.

(En el mar de la mujer
pocos naufragan de noche;
muchos, al amanecer.)

That is, in *thinking* of his love in the clear light, it becomes a
labyrinthine problem. The problem even involves the ugly feeling
of jealousy; the poet confesses to suffering the image of seeing
the beloved talking to twenty others on the "street of jealousy."
Plagued by "evil dreams," he is lost in a labyrinth of confusion,
and even in the last poem of the series he finds no way out of
the desperate situation.

III   *The Poems for Guiomar*

To accompany the basically prose sections of the *Apocryphal Songbook*, in which he provided a metaphysical base, Machado ultimately assembled a small collection of lyric poems, on the three themes of love, God, and death, indicating they were "in the manner of" Martín or Juan de Mairena. Specifically relating to the love theme, and thus to the experience with Guiomar, are the long and difficult poem called "Recollections of Dream, Fever and Fitful Sleep" (CLXXII) and a series entitled "Songs to Guiomar" (CLXXIII). Significantly, Machado himself placed these poems together, although the first is of much broader implications than the lyrics to Guiomar.

"Recollections of Dream, Fever and Fitful Sleep," carefully orchestrated in twelve sections, is perhaps Machado's most impressive single poem, although certainly not his most typical.[8] The poem is the poet's anguished cry (indeed, the nearest he ever came to a howl) at the insufficiency, injustice, confusion, and horror of life. It was written around 1928, for him a time of feverish production, of great promise but massive disappointment also. The newer generation of poets was deserting his kind of poetry, and Machado stubbornly tried to persist in the old way; yet in this poem he makes a concession by shifting in form to the artistic heptasyllabic line, a form favored by the new poets. The newer Freudian psychology seemed to be making obsolete the older way of looking at life. But Machado, who before used the dream in the sense of reverie, actually adopts the Freudian manner of exploring dreams. The poem is supposedly a dream sequence, with all the embroiling of time and experience, hopes, and especially fears which a real dream involves.

The poem begins in a fever of a strange kind:

> This accursed fever
> That has me gripped and shaken,
> Always shouting, "Clear!"
> Asleep you are: Awaken.

> *(Esta maldita fiebre*
> *que todo me lo enreda,*
> *siempre diciendo: ¡claro!*
> *Dormido estás: despierta.*

Of course the only clear thing in a feverish dream is the fact of confusion, but the poet goes on to reiterate a refrain which becomes constant: "Oh, clear, clear, clear." The obvious fact in the first section is that the "unfulfilled wish" of the dream involves a lady: "I come before your window / Bearing a fresh-cut rose." But in his dream this emotional experience becomes embroiled: Inés, Lucía, and Carmela are all one. In this dream the poet suggests a stripping away of all reticence. The whole second section is a single, inclusive line: "Upon the naked earth." In section III, his memory drifts back to Soria and the wind-driven snow there; for a moment he sees, "Upon the towers of oblivion," a feminine figure, surely a fleeting suggestion of his departed wife.

As the scene shifts in section IV, the poet is alone with an "executioner." Actually Machado utilizes here the products of a "nightmare" he jotted down in 1914, still agonizing from his wife's death. The scene is one of "guilt"; the poet as a "gentleman" prefers to be beheaded, but the executioner insists on the common method of hanging. And what is the poet's "crime," which must be one common to mankind? Although he dares not state it, it must concern his forbidden love for Guiomar, who was in fact married. Suddenly the victim discovers he is also a "heretic," clothed in the robes of disgrace. Thus the poet's strong ethical sense asserts itself; he has sinned against both society and the Church. In section V, there is a distant sound of a pack of hounds, surely the hounds of conscience.

That the "unfulfilled wish" of the dream concerns love is further proved by section VI, a fine lyrical stanza in which he reverts to his typical form. Along a clear path, he says, near the "cold waters" there is a "tiny tree," a tree whose fruit only the child knows—no adult has ever seen its flower. This tree has a special purpose:

> That tiny treelet grows
> For only the winged creature of a date,
> Which is soul—song and plumes—of an instant,
> A tiny bluebird small and petulant,
> Who visits it when afternoon grows late.
>
> *(Ese arbolillo crece*
> *no más que para el ave de una cita,*

que es alma—canto y plumas—de un instante,
un pajarillo azul y petulante
que a la hora de la tarde lo visita.)

The poet has already declared that the fruition of love is even metaphysically impossible. This "petulant" bluebird brings only a "message" of love; his song (the poetry) is the only product that abides.

After this scene, the poet, retreating almost into burlesque, projects the "jocund thought" of jumping astride the world, stopping it, and spinning it backwards, reversing time which has gone for him. Then he descends in section IX into Hell itself where in a Dantesque scene he is given a guided tour through the maze of streets there. This metaphor of the streets is developed at length; the poet wanders down the streets of his own experience. Beginning on Remembrance Street, he pauses by the "Square of the White Nun" (a suggestion of the sanctified memory of his wife); then near Oblivion Street, and by way of the cross street of Love, he finally reaches the Plaza of the Final Disenchantment.

But his sad journey is not yet over. In the powerful last section (XII), continuing the street imagery, he brings together all the threads of the previous scenes. He begins with a chilling conclusion:

Oh, clear, clear, clear!
Love always turns to ice.

(Oí claro, claro, claro!
Amor siempre se hiela.)

Here, for once, the usually ironic refrain is no longer ironic, but ominously true. Love has become a Long Street, and there are a few areas still to traverse. "Love is a street entire," and on Long Street the poet is plagued by the nightmarish vision of seeing the beloved chatting with a "hundred gallants" at the window grills. Nearby is the Plaza Where the Old Crone Spins; the old one is, of course, Death herself. In this place of utter desperation lives a "mad priest" pining for an "adolescent lad" (probably the aging poet pining after youth, not a religious criticism). The final street is the Street of the Sad Cruet (apparently Prostitution Street). But the essentially noble poet cries halt at this point; he prefers to dream of the beloved as dead rather than to profane any aspect of their relationship. Unable to pray, he tells his guide in Hell that he refuses to wander farther in the maze of streets which are his human problem, and concludes ironically with the only certainty left to him: "Yes, two and two make four."

"Recollections of Dream, Fever and Fitful Sleep" is a hard and bitter poem. Obviously contemporary, it implies social and religious criticism, but its central emphasis is the insufficiency of life itself, an insufficiency Machado proved with his own metaphysics. Although often steeped in anguish, Machado nevertheless was usually a poet of control. Even here the form is tightly controlled and admirably developed; but the substance of the poem is feverish, anguished, desperate. Read in conjunction with his other lyrics of deep human emotion, this complex poem is surely his greatest.

With the passage of a year or two, the poet, living with "absence and distance," regains his control and creates his specific "Songs for Guiomar" (CLXXIII, CLXXIV) over a period of years. This series projects his yearning overwhelmed by sad hopelessness, but his voice rings out clearly and firmly. When the possibility of a love between Guiomar and the poet suddenly appeared (we are never told the initial situation), he is puzzled because of the unusual circumstances:

> I knew not what
> Your hand held out to me,
> Was it a lemon ripe,
> Or the thread of lucid day
> From a golden skein, Guiomar?
> Your mouth smiled at me.
>
> *(No sabía*
> *si era un limón amarillo*
> *lo que tu mano tenía,*
> *o el hilo de un claro día,*
> *Guiomar, en dorado ovillo.*
> *Tu boca me sonría.)*

Was this love to be "time in fruit" which Guiomar, already a mature woman, was offering, or "vain time" of an afternoon already past? Was it to be "Golden enchanted absence," an ideal inspiration without physical presence? Was it to break the "turbid mirror" of the poet's self-enforced solitude?

For all too brief a moment the poet believes in the physical presence of Guiomar. Apparently he was with her once while she was on vacation at one of the seaside resorts in Northern Spain, and he recorded one of these moments of specific physical attraction.

> And in the flowing sand
> Along the shore
> Your dark, rose-tinted flesh,
> Suddenly, Guiomar!
>
> *(Y en la tersa arena,*
> *cerca de la mar,*
> *tu carne rosa y morena,*
> *Súbitamente, Guiomar.)*

As a poet, the chaste Machado never went further than this, although he unburdened himself in private letters and behind the safety of his ironic philosophical prose.

In the security of his reveries, he dreams a fairy-tale ending for their love story by imagining them upon a trip, beginning perhaps in Segovia where they met and crossing the Guadarrama Mountains—a journey he knew well. But this is a journey out of time and place, beyond the restrictions of society and even the pursuit of God Himself:

> For a goddess and her prince
> Are together fleeing . . .
> Beyond the granite mountains,
> Basaltic mountains beyond,
> Ocean and infinity,
> We go together free.
> Though God, a wrathful King
> As in the fairy tales,
> Mount charger like the wind,
> Though He swear violently
> On us His curse,
> Although He saddle thought,
> None overtakes love free.
>
> *(Porque una diosa y su amante*
> *huyen juntos . . .*

> *Tras los montes de granito*
> *y otros montes de basalto,*
> *ya es la mar y el infinito.*
> *Juntos vamos; libres somos.*
> *Aunque el Dios, como en el cuento*
> *fiero rey, cabalgue a lomos*
> *del mejor corcel del viento,*
> *aunque nos jure, violento,*
> *su venganza,*
> *aunque ensille el pensamiento,*
> *libre amor, nadie lo alcanza.)*

What overtakes Machado's love free is his own pale cast of thought, which inevitably tends to "lose the name of action." In an early lyric in the series, in ballad form, the poet begins to retreat from the world of real experience into his world of the timeless realm of poetry:

> I've dreamed you in a garden high,
> Guiomar, above the river;
> A garden with cold iron grills,
> Closed to time forever.

> *(En un jardín te se soñado,*
> *alto, Guiomar, sobre el río,*
> *jardín de un tiempo cerrado*
> *con verjas de hierro frío.)*

Their love has in fact been a mutual garden "invented" by both the lovers, a dream in which the two have momentarily forgotten the harsh "twin-themed story" which is life:

> One: man and woman,
> Although lion and gazelle
> Come down together to drink.
> The other: Love cannot dwell
> In such good fortune:
> Two solitudes in one,
> Not even of man and woman.

> *(Uno: Mujer y varón,*
> *aunque gacela y león,*
> *llegan juntos a beber.*
> *El otro: No puede ser*
> *amor de tanta fortuna:*
> *dos soledades en una,*
> *ni aun de varón y mujer.)*

Machado is in his element when steeped in absence and distance; he makes his love a "memory" to be explored and caressed:

> Today I write you from my traveller's cell,
> Come now the hour of an imagined date . . .
> All is transparent in this April light;
> All in this today of yesterday, this Yet
> Which in mature hours
> Time sings and stories tells
> Is blended into one melodic line,
> Which is a chorus of afternoons and dawns.
> To you, Guiomar, this deep nostalgia of mine.

> *(Hoy te escribo en mi celda de viajero,*
> *a la hora de una cita imaginaria . . .*
> *Todo a esta luz de abril se transparenta;*
> *todo en el hoy de ayer, el Todavía*
> *que en sus maduras horas*
> *el tiempo canta y cuenta,*
> *se funde en una sola melodía*
> *que es un coro de tardes y de auroras.*
> *A ti, Guiomar, esta nostalgia mía.)*

This nostalgia, this intense yearning toward the other, becomes the only real thing in the poet's existence.

Soon the poet can drift into finely expressed abstractions, still stubbornly supporting the *idea* of love but finding it in practice a creation in the lover's mind:

> All love is fantasy;
> Love invents the day, the year,
> The hour and its melody;
> It invents the lover and moreover,
> The beloved. It nothing proves
> Against love that the beloved one
> Might have existed never.

> *(Todo amor es fantasía;*
> *el inventa el año, el día,*
> *la hora y su melodía;*
> *inventa el amante y, más,*
> *la amada. No prueba nada,*
> *contra el amor, que la amada*
> *no haya existido jamás.)*

This series for Guiomar[9] ends with a powerful sonnet of irregular form, in which Machado projects all his horror and fear and anger before the threat to his temporal existence, a horror relieved only by the fitful appearance of love. His love is symbolized by a "strong butterfly of unpredictable flight," a butterfly which rises from the "horrible carrion" of the "flower of nothingness" in the rose garden itself. This fragile butterfly of love lives under constant threat of extinction, symbolized here by the viper, the lizard, and the toad. As it flies over the sundrenched countryside,

> A spreading fan of miracles has opened wide—
> The angel of lyric song has wished it thus—
> In the creative hand of nothingness . . .
>
> *(Se ha abierto un abanico de milagros*
> *—el ángel del poema la ha querido—*
> *en la mano creadora del olvido . . .)*

The only meaningful event in life is the brief miracle of love, and the only enduring thing is the poetry which that miracle inspires.

IV *Poems for the God of Nothingness*

While stressing the ultimate subjectivity of everything connected with his being or soul, Machado nevertheless felt a persistent urge to overcome that subjectivity by recognizing an incurable yearning toward *Otherness.* In his lyric poetry, this Otherness becomes "erotic" and takes the form of woman, the beloved. In the social sphere, it becomes fraternal love, exemplified clearly in Jesus.[10] In the *Apocryphal Songbook*, the ultimate yearning, religious or metaphysical, is of course toward God. Machado's idea of God is complex, unorthodox, and at times confusing, because he never developed an organized philosophical system. As we have indicated, his idea that the universe is a single monad of active consciousness, *the great eye that sees all on seeing itself*, has a special meaning, because in this seemingly pantheistic concept he does not include God. At one level, God is a being that "we all make," says Machado; that

is, He is a being immanent in the human soul, who outside it
has no reality. This definition seems to exclude, or at least seriously redefines, the Christian God. Martín specifically rejects,
even scorns, the Jewish God, who is a God of procreation;
Machado also rejects the Aristotelian God, the "prime mover
unmoved." In Martín's "theology," God is defined as "the absolute being," but in his ironic manner Martín gradually makes
it clear that this God is so far outside and beyond the consciousness of man that his "absolute being" is in reality Nothingness.
By progression Martín reaches this idea. First, "the concept of
non-being is the specifically human creation," but then this idea
is subtly reversed: "God bequeaths to man the great Zero,
Nothingness . . ."

The all-inclusive sonnet which projects these ideas is entitled
"To the Great Zero," a clear indication that God *is* the Zero, or
nothingness. This complex sonnet begins in devastating irony:

> When the Being who *is* created Nothingness
> And rested (knowing well he earned that rest)
> Then day had its night and man enjoyed
> Companionship in the absence of the beloved.
> *Fiat umbra!* And human thought burst forth.
> And he held the empty, universal egg on high . . .

> *(Cuando el Ser que se es hizo la nada*
> *y reposó, que bien lo merecía,*
> *ya tuvo el día noche, y compañía*
> *tuvo el hombre en la ausencia de la amada.*
> ¡Fiat umbra! *Brotó el pensar humano.*
> *Y el huevo universal alzó, vació . . .)*

This first part of the sonnet, which is obviously a travesty of
the Creation scene in Genesis, projects the actual creation of
nothingness. In analyzing his own sonnet, Martín stresses the
fact that God "bequeaths" the Zero to man so that "the human
mind will possess a concept of totality." The poet has already
declared that man's natural complement is impossible, that "the
beloved is impossible." Therefore God has provided the companionship of nothingness. In the poet's reasoning, his consciousness *is*, and nothing *is not*; therefore, the two complement
each other. In the continuation of the sonnet, the poet faces the
utter bleakness of this human position; as he puts it ironically,

when "the beast's loins became shoulders," when man stood erect, he gained this knowledge. What then can the poet do? As the sonnet concludes, he can sing this fact, chilling as it is, in a song "To death, to silence and to Nothingness."

Machado attempts to push a step further the bleak direction of this sonnet in a final poem on God, entitled "To the Great Plenitude or Total Consciousness." This poem, he says, is a "prologue" (Alas, a prologue to what?) in one of Martín's books. In the beginning, this God, "the uplifted Zero," is reigning eternally on his throne; all the universe is now in "Harmony," a harmony brought about by the final resolution of the problem of being and nothingness. By Machado's complicated reasoning, *being* and *thought* never coincide. Thought leads us to the idea of nothingness. Therefore, once this idea of nothingness is thought fully, the poet can discard it and concentrate on expressing the fullness of Being. This new "poetic dialectic" is supposedly Martín's deepest intuition, though he himself admits the idea is "absurd and paradoxical." In any case, the "Harmony" in this final poem remains a massive irony, and Machado apparently deserts this pursuit of God in despair.

V   *The Poems on Death*

Toward the end of the *Apocryphal Songbook*, there is a small number of impressive poems on death. While Machado lived under the permanent threat and dread of death as the bringer of oblivion, poems on death itself are rare in his work, except for one atypical realistic lyric in *Solitudes* (IV). In the *Apocryphal Songbook*, however, his creation of the *persona* Abel Martín, who supposedly died in 1898, provides him with a death "experienced," at least poetically and imaginatively. Surprisingly, in the *Apocryphal Songbook* Machado does not even mention death in his extensive prose metaphysics, despite the inclusion of the poems; therefore we must provide a meaningful transition from the poet's discussions of being, otherness, God, and nothingness. Since for Machado being is *active* consciousness, naturally a state of rest or final inactivity is equal to death. Or approached in another way, life is temporality, and the poet normally writes from the standpoint that time is a "Yes / pregnant

with imminences." Thus temporality (or life) is the opposite
of the state of death (which is nothingness).

The transition from life to death is suggested, and then aborted, in "Mairena to Martín, Dead" (CLXVIII). There is a tricki-
ness in the temporal relations in the poem in that Mairena and
Martín are both actually dead, but the poet writing is really still
concerned with earthly love. Now it is a "cross-eyed love"; as
the prose explication indicates, Mairena is malevolently scorn-
ing the very ideas his old teacher Martín defended. Thus this
poem breaks down into a "Baroque" sarcasm which is more
rational than emotional.

It is in the "Final Lamentations of Abel Martín" (CLXIX)
where the aging poet begins to make the emotional transition
toward death. Typically, he evokes his state of reverie, and obe-
diently the figure of his youth appears, "a whippet of yesterday." Although "Time and its flying pennants" still exist, like a
ship ready for further adventure, the aging poet seems loathe to
set out. In fact, his heart cries out for rest, rest from the ceaseless activity which for him is life:

> Oh, now to rest lost in the blue of day,
> Just as the eagle rests upon the wind
> Above the mountains cold,
> Sure of his power to ascend!
>
> I ask of you, O Nature,
> An august confidence, tranquility,
> Surcease from dread and hope,
> A grain of joy, and then oblivion's sea.
>
> *(¡Oh, descansar en el azul del día*
> *como descansa el águila en el viento,*
> *sobre la tierra fría,*
> *segura de sus alas y su aliento!*
>
> *La augusta confianza*
> *a ti, Naturaleza, y paz te pido,*
> *mi tregua de temor y de esperanza,*
> *un grano de alegría, un mar de olvido . . .)*

In "Death of Abel Martín" (CLXXV), Machado reaches the
highest moment of emotional intensity in all his work. For the
reader who has patiently absorbed his poetry up to this moment, the opening lines evoke a chill of emotional identification,

although the images (except for the dark martins) are typical
of the poet:

> The last dark martins flutter in profusion
> Around the cathedral tower;
> The children shout, leap, scuffle in confusion.
> And in his corner, Martín in loneliness.
> Dust-laden afternoon, just as the dusk appears—
> The childhood din, his roar of consciousness—
> Their dozen blended with his fifty years!
>
> *(Los últimos vencejos revolean*
> *en torno al campanario;*
> *los niños gritan, saltan, se pelean.*
> *En su rincón, Martín el solitario.*
> *¡La tarde, casi noche, polvorienta,*
> *La algazara infantil, y el vocerío,*
> *a la par, de sus doce en sus cincuenta!)*

But in his final "solitude" which follows, the poet is chilling-
ly alone with the substance of his memories. Of course two
areas of memory stand out. First, there is his pursuit of love,
which he now calls "sacred oblivion." He has followed the
"aloof muse," anxious for a glimpse of her real face; now in his
anguish he suspects she was not what he believed her to be.
And in fact, by a sudden shift of image, she seems to be death
herself. Even more important is his final "great knowledge of
the Zero," his awareness of nothingness, an awareness which
only man "enjoys." Although he has lived, slept, dreamed, and
created a "man who stands watch / Over the dream," a man
who pursues hope of salvation, he still suspects that God's only
creation is "pure nothingness." That is, God is equated with
nothingness; God does not exist outside the heart of man.

In the final scene, human fatigue follows upon his anguish.
His body suffers ultimate enfeeblement, feeling "the bitterness
of envenomed time." Although he utters a cry for salvation,
raising his hand up to the "vermilion light," the light fails and
he is left in darkness. Now comes the serenity of finality:

> Then, with serenity,
> He raised to his cold lips the limpid glass,
> With pure shadow—oh, pure shadow!—filled.

(Luego, llevó, sereno,
el limpio vaso, hasta su boca fría,
de pura sombra—¡oh, pura sombra!—lleno.)

Normally this glass, this vessel of life, would be filled with light or with water, both light and water being symbols of hope and salvation. Martín's vessel, however, more than just in shadow, actually contains a special kind of "pure" shadow. Perhaps the poet intends to suggest that the "pure shadow" is not a corruption of light, but a "pure," positive substance of nothingness.

After the emotional intensity of Martín's death scene, Machado preferred in his official poetic works to conclude with "Another Climate" (CLXXVI), a poem expressing the distance, absence, and quietness so often typical of him. Indeed, the setting is beyond the time and space of this world. The poet, whose "chambers of time and galleries of the soul" are utterly bare, imagines himself far out in the universe, watching the birth and death of worlds. For ours, he sees a *"nihil* of fire written upon the granite crust, / A road lightning-slashed upon the mountain." This road is surely the faintest of promises.

VI   *Conclusion*

In the short second part of the prose discussions in the *Apocryphal Songbook*, in which Juan de Mairena is being reported, there is an organized attack on Spanish Baroque poetry of the seventeenth century. What Machado is actually doing is using Baroque poetry as an excuse to attack the vanguard poetry of the 1920's. As an insistently "temporal" poet, Machado waged a personal battle against both Baroque and vanguard poetry for the same reason: that both were conceptual, artificial and, above all, not intuitive. As we know, Machado thought of poetry as the expression of intimate, personal experience.

Of even more serious consequences is the clever dialogue which ends the prose section of the *Apocryphal Songbook*. Our contemporary age—he says through his third *persona* Jorge Meneses—with its emphasis on mass man and mechanical materialism, has made individual sentiment superfluous and ineffective as matter for poetry. What is needed is a way to express the collective, mechanized sentiment of our time. Jorge Meneses has responded to this need by inventing a "poetry machine," a kind of hand organ with the talents of our modern computers. The poet feeds into the computer meaningful terms such as *man* and *woman*, and out comes a *copla* supposedly suitable for mass man. But the insistence on these terms man and woman arouses our suspicions, when we recall the *copla* from which Martín extracted all his metaphysics at the beginning of the *Apocryphal Songbook*. And indeed, when Meneses feeds the computer, out comes the *copla* of the expected love theme:

> 'Tis said man is not man
> Unless his name he see
> Upon the lips of woman.
> It could well be.
>
> *(Dicen que el hombre no es hombre*
> *mientras que no oye su nombre*
> *de labios de una mujer.*
> *Puede ser.)*

Thus, for the third time Antonio Machado marks the end of a period of poetic creation with an expressed defeat. At the end of *Solitudes*, he lamented the fact that his poetic intuition was becoming philosophical speculation; toward the end of *Fields of Castile*, he was retreating into solitude and into the philosophy of his "Proverbs and Songs." This time his expression of defeat as a poet is almost total, for he predicts nothing less than the disappearance of the lyric poet. He expects nothing from the intellectual poetry then being discussed, and he has only faint hope in a poetry for the masses—or, as he would say, people. For Machado, who matured at a time when belief in lyric poetry was almost an article of faith, it must have been a bitter blow to see another of his worlds collapsing in the later years of his life. Despite the fact that his three journeys into poetry were followed by withdrawals in defeat, his own poetry of course has continued to live, almost as fresh and human as when he dreamed it. His gloomy predictions on the future of poetry have proved to be prophetic, however, for the lyric poet of our day seems to be encountering an increasingly indifferent world.

CHAPTER 5

Philosophy in the Service of Man:
Juan de Mairena

IN the previous chapter we have seen how Machado's first important *persona*, Abel Martín, as poet and metaphysician first intuited some tiny *coplas*, elaborated a metaphysics upon them, and then produced a group of intense, profound, and disturbing poems. Even before the end of the *Apocryphal Songbook*, however, as the "erotic," the poetic in Abel Martín began to fade into the old age of his creator, Machado returned to his philosophical reflections and transferred them to his second *persona*, Juan de Mairena. Mairena, who had first turned up in an Andalusian *copla* around 1917, retains to the end some touches of his popular origin. In the *Apocryphal Songbook* he is described as a poet, philosopher, and rhetorician, in that order. By 1934, Machado is ready to reestablish Juan de Mairena as a character who is essentially a professor with a strong bent toward philosophy and rhetoric. Even as a character, however, Mairena is inextricably entangled with Machado and with Abel Martín, for he often declares he is only reporting his teacher Abel Martín and sometimes slips in personal details relating to Machado.

Around 1934, Machado, now nearly sixty and (he said) old for a Spaniard, seemed to be vegetating in a monotonous existence in Madrid. In his silent way he made his shuffling journey from his humble room to his classes at the Institute and to the long *tertulias* in the cafés. It must have surprised many, then, when a Madrid journal began to publish the philosophical meanderings of Juan de Mairena. In 1936, Machado published a collection of these articles under the title of *Juan de Mairena*, with a long subtitle, "Maxims, Witticisms, Notes and Remembrances of an Apocryphal Professor." During the three years of the Civil War, he continued the series in basically the same manner, with only traces of propaganda. In the *Works* these two series have been logically placed together, to form a volume of about 240 pages with an essential unity. Somewhat typical of Spanish books, the work is difficult to classify. It is almost completely open-ended in structure, with no real beginning or end. Only the character of Mairena, who has a certain consistency in his ideas and manner, holds the elements loosely together. Occasionally Mairena's trenchant observations are compressed into a paragraph, or even a maxim in one sentence. Above all, the subtitle suggests that Mairena is a *character* who is specifically a professor, though assuredly an untypical one.

Juan de Mairena is Antonio Machado's creation of the ideal professor, and he undoubtedly worked from many models. The oldest is of course Socrates, the proponent of the use of rational thought to pursue knowledge and truth. In his human qualities, Mairena suggests the educator Francisco de Giner. But it was probably Unamuno who served as Machado's immediate model. Machado admired Unamuno almost to idolatry, because of his great knowledge and his ability to arouse sleeping consciences. Ultimately, of course, Mairena expresses the qualities of mind and character which Machado himself had been developing over thirty years.

Juan de Mairena, in spite of a professed modesty, is nevertheless a character who creates and guards an individuality, a quirk which reminds us of the minor eccentricities of the members of the Generation of 98. Thus Unamuno wore his clerical collars, Baroja his *boina* (the beret of Northern Spain), and Azorín carried his red umbrella. Antonio Machado almost made a cult of sloppiness in dress, a fact which prompted Unamuno to remark once, "There goes the man with the most slovenly exterior and the cleanest soul I've ever known." Machado's Juan de Mairena is himself given to wearing a ratty old overcoat of such "personality" that he is even able to extract philosophy from it. He calls it his "Catalan vengeance," because its unique fabric ("which weighs a lot and shelters but little") is made in the province of Catalonia. The fabric of the coat so attracts dust that Mairena, after much meditation, dreamed up a kind of brush for it, a cross between a brush and a type of "flypaper." Since the fabric was so badly made, however, the brush was a miserable failure: at the same time the brush removed dust, it

destroyed the fabric, literally turning it to dust. This wry episode of the "Catalan vengeance" of course has a moral. Mairena
goes on to say that his overcoat is like Western culture in his
day: it weighs a lot but shelters little, though many zealously
want to preserve it. He stands divided: He could bear to have it
taken away, but he thinks that no one will dispute his privilege
of wearing it all his days.[1]

In essence, Mairena is a gentle skeptic, given to ironic humor
out of modesty, but he has his *malas pulgas*, his "bad fleas" as
the Spaniards say, and this tendency toward wrath, which
bursts forth only rarely, is usually aroused by the unbudging
inertia of the conservative. In one scene, Mairena, who has a
reputation for giving impossibly brief oral examinations, has
failed a student after a typical one of a few cursory questions.
When the lad's father comes to the school and rightfully pro-
tests, Mairena churlishly tells him that often just by seeing the
father he will know the son is a blockhead.[2] Although Mairena
is older, in an intimate moment he confesses that he has not
really gone from "gallant to graybeard," but has grown toward
a youthfulness. His ideal professional situation springs from an
irony and a rebellion. Officially he is a professor of physical education (a discipline which his creator Machado detested); he becomes a professor of rhetoric by establishing an unofficial seminar with no attendance requirements and no set curriculum. His
seminars proceed in a leisurely fashion, the way Socrates used
to conduct one, with the leader doing most of the talking. Yet
in the back of his teeming mind, Mairena is envisioning sweep-
ing educational and social reforms, along the lines of the
Generation of 98.

Since Juan de Mairena is a free professor with a class of vol-
unteers, he is at liberty to introduce a wide variety of materials.
He comments critically on poetry, drama, criticism, politics, education, folklore, religion, nationalism, metaphysics, skepticism
—wherever his fancy takes him. Often these comments synthe-
size Machado's study and thought of a lifetime. Mairena is interested in the great figures of Western culture: Heraclitus, Demo-
critus, Socrates, Plato, Descartes, Kant, Shakespeare, Cervantes,
Tolstoy, Marx, Nietzsche, Schopenhauer, Bergson, Heidegger,
etc. He also expresses some carefully pondered and pertinent

observations regarding Spanish figures, such as Unamuno, Valle-Inclán, Espronceda, Bécquer, Zorrilla, Lope de Vega, Calderón de la Barca, and others. Yet he can use such disparate characters as an obscure bullfighter named Badila, the American boxer Jack Johnson, and the owner of a sweetshop named Angel Martínez to draw salient conclusions on philosophical subjects. Although a number of the themes are developed at length, Machado usually prefers the single trenchant paragraph with a single idea; there is often a complete change of subject between paragraphs. One of the outstanding characteristics of *Juan de Mairena* is its surprising variety; it can be dipped into at any point and enjoyed, sometimes in relation to Spain and Western culture, sometimes for the light cast upon the personality and work of Mairena—that is, Machado himself.

I   *The Central Themes of* Juan de Mairena

While many of the great ideas of Western civilization are mentioned at some point within this wide diversity of materials, it is possible to focus upon certain essential themes. Certainly we must understand first that Mairena is a confirmed skeptic who even doubts doubt; the whole book is pervaded with a sense of irony. Mairena thinks profoundly, but, in typical Spanish fashion, without a complete system; in fact, he declares himself to be a man of his times, and "the peculiar characteristic of our age is living in complete contradiction."[3] His book is therefore one of "notes" rather than systems; however, in spite of a lack of formal order, certain important sections emphasize Mairena's central ideas and preoccupations.

In his cryptic way, Mairena actually begins the book with a projection of this sense of contradiction. First, there is a grand assertion: "Truth is truth, whether Agamemnon or his swineherd utter it." In the miniscule dialogue which follows, Agamemnon replies: "Agreed." The swineherd, however, is skeptical: "I am not convinced."[4] Although these are ancient figures, clearly suggested is the modern idea that truth and ideas are no longer the province of the privileged few. The rise of the common man, the growing right of every individual to assert himself has become a fact in our century. Of course the swineherd's questioning of authority, as the skeptic Mairena knows, involves *all* authority, be it just or unjust. Any ideas or truths of the so-called ruling class must be applicable to, and must convince, the whole social body. Moreover, Mairena must be suggesting that the modern emphasis upon the individual makes it difficult for him to accept the "truth" of another. Finally, given Mairena's belief that his being is immersed in the irreversible flow of time, the whole concept of uttering general truths becomes a doubtful process. Of course Mairena's opening dialogue, merely puzzling and provocative initially, takes on its full meaning during the course of the book.

In Section XXV of the first part,[5] Mairena introduces a discussion of great general importance. He ironically analyzes his seminar as "a kind of philosophical astrakhan." This word *astracán* refers to a type of play not quite respectable in the literary world, a popular play of grotesque, burlesque, and humorous elements. Thus Mairena humorously belittles his seminar, but in the same paragraph goes on to assert its great importance. He and his class are students of Rhetoric, which in the ancient sense is the art of speaking and writing well. But, he asks, how can one speak well without thinking well? Focus on thinking leads him to logic, to a study of the habits of thought which makes possible the knowing of something. By logic Mairena means the logic of Aristotle (or Socrates) and the Greeks. And in this section, as well as in many others, Mairena rejects the Greek system of logic, sometimes even poking fun at it. He specifically rejects the elements of the syllogism; for him things have no opposites, no real similarities, nor any expressible relation to each other. Premises and conclusions cannot coexist.

Mairena's logic purports to be that of "a poetic thinking." His specific reference to his old master Abel Martín, and his use of the word "poetic," alert us to the fact that he is bringing up his idea of "being in time," a concept we discussed in the last chapter. Mairena's logic is a "thinking in time"; time itself is a "pure irreversible succession." In this logic he also goes from "the one to the other," another idea we have already explored. Mairena considers that this *being in time* is absolutely unique; therefore any comparison or contrast with any other being or thing is impossible and worthless. Perhaps it is hair-splitting, but Mairena insists that a premise uttered at one point in time, followed by a conclusion necessarily uttered at another point in time, cannot have any validity.

Immediately on enunciating this "temporal" logic, Mairena, with his usual irony, confesses that it is "more or less unrealizable." Certainly his untrained students are not ready for "poetic logic," and must serve their apprenticeship, doing battle with syllogistic thinking, popular illogic, and "the verbal confusion of drunks." In the next section,[6] he introduces a long syllogistic nightmare in which he attempts to prove that, since man invented clothes to protect the beauty of nakedness, by analogy he invented the cage to protect the liberty of the bird. When the students become thoroughly confounded, he tells them perhaps they can improve their understanding only by improving their "understander." Having thus demolished the traditional method of applying the intelligence at this point, he can still conclude at another: "Our mission is to advance by means of the intelligence toward returning the dignity of man to the human animal."[7]

The sense of contradiction in our age is further exemplified by his discussion of belief in the absolutes and belief in complete relativism. Mairena has strong words regarding the absolute: "When man stops believing in the absolute, he then believes in nothing. Because all belief is belief in the absolute. Everything else is called thinking."[8] Although Mairena himself does a lot of thinking, he returns again and again to belief in the absolutes, not from the Christian tradition, but from the philosophy of Plato and his doctrine of the ideas or universals—truth, justice, beauty, etc. He deplores the fact that in his time this point of view seems not to be a living concern, and he insists on vitalizing Plato in his classroom even to his young charges. Of course Plato and the Greeks projected these universals by utilizing their discovery of logic or rational thought. At this point, however, Mairena reserves his scorn for the pragmatists, in general the enemies of Platonism. He recoils especially against that part of pragmatist doctrine which preaches that we should adopt as true whatever proves to be useful. Mairena's attraction to the absolutes is sincere, though his acceptance of them is filled with contradictions. For example, one of his greatest ironies involves his inability to believe in the idea of God as an absolute, and he consequently reversed the traditional idea of God as everything and made Him a God of Nothingness.

Mairena's religious ideas are generally unorthodox, if not downright blasphemous, especially in relation to the Catholic culture in which he lived. In no sense an isolated case, his is typical of the Generation of 98, which, led by Unamuno, was the first in Spain to attack or reinterpret traditional Catholicism. Mairena is deeply attracted to the figure of Jesus, but his ideas of Him are certainly not the traditional ones. In approaching two of the great streams in Western culture, Mairena declares that "the Platonic faith," or Platonism, is "a faith in the metaphysical reality of the idea, which the centuries have not succeeded in destroying."[9] But, insists Mairena in his human and personal way, the greatness of Platonism is "not sufficient to cure the loneliness of man." This was the deed of Christ, a "Promethean act" which in a certain sense is Satanic. As Mairena understands it, the deed is both Promethean and Satanic, for he clearly enunciates the idea that "Christ was a man who became (or made himself) God in order to expiate upon the Cross the great sin of the Divinity." The "Sin" of the Jewish God concerns the emphasis upon mere procreation of the race. Mairena's appreciation of the Hebraic stream in Western culture is extremely limited, and he never tires of repeating the Jewish emphasis upon continuing the race. Moreover, Mairena has hard and unfeeling words for all the Bible, except for a few passages in the Gospels. Rebelling against this God, Jesus teaches that there is a "Father, father of all," a "transcendent erotic object" which becomes the seat and sum of human fraternity.

Mairena insists stubbornly upon emphasizing his unorthodox ideas concerning Christ. In one of the final sections of *Juan de Mairena*, with the pretense of commenting upon a recent article, he reveals his final independent conclusions. After Unamuno's unorthodox speculations, he declares, there is the possibility of developing a Christian philosophy in Spain in which "Christ is not buried again in Aristotle."[10] By this phrase Mairena seems to mean a Christ of philosophical abstraction. But, insists Mairena, finally asserting his independence of Unamuno, "Unamuno did not restore Christ to his true cross." Unamuno, like St. Paul, preferred to dwell upon the Crucified, the agonizing Christ.

Unamuno's long poem, *El Cristo de Velázquez*, is a meditation upon the stark painting of Christ upon the cross by Velázquez. Mairena, calling himself a "heretic," wants to "plant Christ's feet again upon the earth." Mairena's Christ therefore becomes a human figure, with God immanent in his heart; his Christ possesses infinitely that "essential heterogeneity of being," the incurable "nostalgia toward otherness," an immeasurable brotherly love. The ultimate consequence of this idea of Christ is that he becomes a human figure, that God exists only *in becoming* in his heart and, as a consequence, the traditional God no longer exists. Paradoxical as it sounds (and today it sounds less so), Mairena wants to free Christ from the Church and return him to the "people," though admittedly his definition of people remained something of an abstraction.

Given his special idea of the "divinity" of Christ, Mairena, in another discussion on another day of class, continues to pursue the great problem of a definition of God. Let us imagine, he says, a post-Aristotelian theology that conceives of God as a great consciousness into which our own consciousnesses (or souls) are "plugged." In this theory the temporal, psychic time, would be essential, and God would share the "anguish" or the "great nostalgia" that the Other suffers for the One. (One of Machado's most persistent philosophical arguments, as we have discussed, concerns this "essential heterogeneity of being.") Thus God would be assigned the eternal task of ceasing to be, or becoming, the other. Mairena lets the class auditor criticize this idea: such a God, totally immersed in time, condemned to live like us minute by minute, would have the "temper of the very demons." Even Mairena backs away from this idea, which he calls a "pantheistic" God, and says the Church rightly condemned it, but he has brought up this "essentially temporal theology because he sees it on the European horizon.[11] (Although he does not identify any sources, perhaps he is referring to German thinkers such as Schleiermacher, Feuerbach, and Scheler.) Certainly Mairena was prophetic, for in our day the "Death of God" theologians have continued to develop such a theology.

Mairena is consistently a man of his own times who has assimilated Western tradition. Perhaps stimulated in his mature years by Ortega's discussions of rationalism, he has studied Plato,

Aristotle, Descartes, and the exponents of rational thought down to Kant, who of course is credited with proving the impossibility of pure reason. Mairena has been fascinated by rational thought, but his thought has been the source of his anguish. In his simple human way he concludes, "Our thought is sad."[12] And why? Mairena's thought leads him inevitably to the idea that God's greatest creation is the creation of nothingness. As he put it in a *copla*: "God said: Let there be nothingness."[13] Mairena reaches this conclusion by the logic that if God can create something, he can also create nothingness; and this nothingness suggests specifically the annihilation of Mairena's *being*. His concept of being is essentially Bergson's idea of intuition, of a consciousness of being through participation. Somewhat desperately, Mairena strives to separate *being* from *thought*; he trusts, in his words, "that being and thought never coincide even by chance."[14] Here is another of his massive ironies: How can he separate being from thought without utilizing the very logic he has rejected?

Although Juan de Mairena is intensely interested in abstract ideas, his overriding concern is to set in motion a system which will utilize ideas to enhance the dignity of man. As he states it simply: "We are inclined to believe in the dignity of man."[15] He emphasizes the point that the specifically human in man is the desire to be other than what he is, to better his essential self, to save himself. Mairena confesses that "not even in dreams" has he been able to escape the moral or ethical bent of his nature. Mairena's program has perhaps two philosophical bases: his belief in "the essential heterogeneity of being" and his communal belief in the Castilian maxim, "Nobody is more than anybody else." Whenever possible, he exalts the folk wisdom of his people, especially that of Andalusia and Castile.

In his pondering upon the nature of Jesus, Mairena gradually develops another idea relating to the dignity of man. On earth before, says Mairena, "Christ preached humility to the powerful; whenever he returns, he will preach pride to the humble."[16] He thus envisions the possibility of dignity for man, for *every* man. In a sense he is expanding Nietzsche's idea of the superman; however, Mairena's superior man is to rise, not by riding roughshod over the masses, but by ethical and cultural development made available to all. In all Mairena's thought there exists the dream of the ideal man, a dream formulated by the developers of the philosophy of *Krausismo* in Spain, among them Francisco Giner and the Free Institute. It is interesting to observe how, in spite of the growth of materialism in the nineteenth century, men such as Carlyle, Emerson, Thoreau, Nietzsche in his particular way, Giner, Unamuno, and Machado's Mairena struggled to keep alive the concept of the ideal man.

Since he considers himself a teacher, Mairena dreams of establishing a "Popular School of Superior Wisdom" to propagate his ideals.[17] The professors of this school will be "extraordinary men," capable of lifting up by their own efforts "the whole sack of wisdom." Thus, while Mairena respects science, he will not utilize specialists in science, however intelligent they may be. Nor will the professors be researchers and antiquarians, interested mainly in history. The professors of this school will largely ignore the practical and the pragmatic in education and concentrate on developing the souls, the consciousness of its pupils. If the professors of this school, the "extraordinary men," will be select and indeed rare, what of the pupils? Mairena does not dream of educating "the masses," he prefers to educate "man." Now Mairena is aware that Ortega y Gasset has popularized the idea of masses and a "select minority," clearly stressing the importance of the select minority. Mairena surely recognizes that any social thinker must work with groups, but he refuses to admit the concept of masses. How can we add up souls, he asks? Actually Mairena is here playing with logic (a retreat he utilizes in the face of a difficult problem); his insistence upon the worth of the individual soul is really a thing of the heart, so that his logic and method break down when he must relate man to a group. Although his little extra-curricular seminar seems a meager beginning, he of course dreams of a striking growth of this personalized approach to teaching until it becomes the revolutionary new educational system in Spain.

For an example of the kind of system he was pondering, Mairena has been drawn to Russian literature and the great Russian social experiment.[18] Rather early Mairena discovered in Dostoevsky and in Tolstoy kindred souls that impressed him deeply. Although the older Russian authors were generally of

the upper class, they "suffered for all the people." Dostoevsky
and Tolstoy dreamed of and agitated for a universal brotherhood
of all men, sustained by the moral fervor of each individual.
During the same period, of course, the economic doctrines of
Karl Marx gained strength. The Russian Revolution attempted
to put these ideas into practice, and "Brotherhood" became the
slogan upon everyone's lips. Mairena has pondered the Russian
experiment with hope and uneasiness, because, along with some
evidences of Christian brotherhood, the Marxist system seems
to be reducing the people to economic and material ciphers.
Mairena continues to preach (and hope) that the Christian tradition of universal brotherhood enunciated by Tolstoy will re-
assert itself, while in fact the Marxist economic emphases
gradually grow stronger. Mairena of course hopes to see a successful revolution in Spanish society, a revolution in which the
reinvigoration of spiritual values triumphs over the inertia and
materialistic concerns of the reigning political groups. However,
Mairena's eyes are open to the fact that his dream faces great
dangers, for in one of his finest paragraphs he analyzes the
"gigantic wave of cynicism" which is threatening the whole
Western world.

This complex paragraph[19] begins with a powerful topic sentence: "A gigantic wave of cynicism threatens the entire world."
By "cynicism" Mairena (emphasizing the etymology of the
word) means a certain faith in human animality (the physical)
over against the "more authentic values" of culture. Certainly
today this wave is upon us in full force, as even the man in the
street can see. This conflict between culture and animality is
typical during the decline of civilizations, according to Mairena.
Tracing the origin of cynicism in our culture back to Rousseau,
he insists that Marx's *materialistic interpretation of history* is
the present version of cynicism. Now normally Mairena would
rise up in wrath against cynicism in this sense, but here he proceeds with subtlety in another direction. A "little cynical" himself, Mairena says that authentic cynicism is "a fanatic cult of
veracity, which does not back up when confronted by the bit-
terest truths about man." Here the enemy becomes the "hypo-
critical pragmatists," by which he means what we now call the
Establishment, and these pragmatists make a cynical reaction

necessary. Obviously Mairena was prophetic, for the two emphases upon man's animality (or the physical) and the omnipresence of hypocrisy (real or imagined) have become two of the salient themes in our time.

II   *Some of Mairena's More Personal Themes*

Although Mairena is usually exploring the ideas of others, occasionally he introduces his own projects. By his own admission, the aging thinker has grown towards a youthfulness, so that it is not surprising that he is keenly interested in the relations between the sexes. He reveals that among his many papers is a "tragicomedy" entitled *The Grand Climax*, to which he refers briefly a number of times.[20] Mairena, in what is a palpable untruth, declares that this tragicomedy shows no influence of Freud. Yet it is a play, in twenty-one acts, which represents a character who symbolizes the unconscious libido from adolescence until the sexual drive ceases—as Mairena sardonically observes, when man "has one foot in the grave." The protagonist is on the stage through all the acts; Mairena insists that in this way he can avoid the usual frivolous dialogue which does not develop the essential theme. Moreover, having studied Shakespeare recently, he has in his play gone back to the use of the soliloquy and the aside. In *The Grand Climax*, Mairena is obviously fascinated by "the voice of the subconscious," which he thinks he has utilized in it. He keeps promising the class to which he is lecturing that he will present some actual scenes, but as is usual when he approaches an insoluble or a personal problem, he retreats behind a stock phrase, "Let that be for another day."

Obviously Mairena has difficulties in establishing real contact with other men, even when the goal is the creation of schools and a new society of brotherhood. Some of the most poignant moments in the book occur when Mairena (and hence Machado) is touching upon aspects of his persistent isolation and loneliness, his "essential heterogeneity of being." In one of his summarizing paragraphs, he begins: "We live in a world essentially apocryphal, in a cosmos or poem of our own thought, all of it ordered or constructed upon undemonstrable supposi-

tions . . ."[21] The most important supposition, he says, is that
by the mere act of thinking things we can make them immuta-
ble, that we can "anchor them in the river of Heraclitus." The
apocryphal nature of our world (for Mairena this favorite word
"apocryphal" means the imagined, the illusory) is proved by the
existence of logic, "by the necessity of putting thought in agreement with itself." Of course, admits Mairena, the thought that
all our suppositions are false is infinitely disturbing. Here again
is the sense of contradiction in which Mairena lives and moves:
in spite of his sincere belief in the brotherhood of man (he is
even willing to deny the divine aspects of Jesus' nature to emphasize the idea of brotherhood), he is constantly reverting to a
state of solipsism in which all other human beings become merely "apocryphal."

As a final personal note, Mairena (and thus Machado) confesses that he has thought seriously about a problem which pre-
occupied his whole generation, especially Unamuno. Should
man work to develop his individual soul, or to create art—in this
case literary works? As a young man, Machado discovered in
Unamuno's passionate writings the idea that the creation of the
individual soul should be man's most important pursuit. However, Unamuno himself later was assailed by doubts and began
to conceive of the world as "theater," that is, a place in which a
man "created himself," thus achieving a kind of immortality.
Now, from the vantage point of his sixty years, Mairena's skepticism begins to arise: "That every man is superior to his work is
the illusion that should be maintained while one is alive." But
he adds: "It is very possible, however, that the contrary is the
truth."[22] Again it is pertinent to point out the new problems of
Machado's skeptical generation. A staunch Catholic such as the
seventeenth-century Cervantes could express no such problem:
for him all the things of this world were ephemeral, including
man's works of art. But when Machado's generation lost its faith
in things eternal, temporal things assumed critical importance.
Therefore Mairena, the skeptic, naturally vacillates, advising his
students "to guard the illusion" that man is superior to his
work, although the suspicion will remain that the contrary is
true. In any case, he exhorts them never to be satisfied with
either their manhood or their work.

In his role as skeptical professor, Mairena casts his critical eye upon everything around him. Therefore, since the series is continued over a lengthy period, it is inevitable that he turn his skepticism, his penetrating criticism, upon himself and his teachings. Certainly Mairena aspires to be the ideal professor, using as a guide the ideas of Giner's *krausismo* as developed in the Institución Libre, and indeed many of these ideas are comparable to our modern ones in America in regard to effective professors. Since he has always believed, Mairena says with a tinge of irony, that confession before our fellow man (priest, doctor, teacher, friend, or public) is a way of cleansing the soul and discovering the best parts of the spirit, he submits himself to an examination of conscience toward the end of *Juan de Mairena*. That he has been indulgent as a professor is a simple error of little consequence, but, he insists, "Our errors are deep, and it is in ourselves where we discover them."[23]

In his examination of conscience, Mairena discovers "two unpardonable faults." One of these involves his moral stature, his right to criticize; he considers himself guilty of "casting the first stone." Certainly the point is true: Mairena *is* guilty of casting stones (and large ones) at the Church, the government, and the upper class (the *señoritos*). We in the last third of our century are likely to find his sense of guilt puzzling because almost any ideas of reform receive a sympathetic hearing. Obviously Mairena is aware that the reformer must operate by attacking existing institutions. But while the Spaniards have been critical of themselves (and bitterly so) at one level, Mairena's generation was the first to be devastatingly critical of all the major institutions at their base. Therefore, when he looks back at the "seminars" he has made public in print, some twinges of doubt emerge concerning the rightness of the reforming ideas.

Mairena's other "unpardonable fault" is probably more serious in regard to his book *Juan de Mairena* and its plans for reform. Mairena confesses that, in spite of his belief in dialogue between individuals, with his students he has been "anti-Socratic"; he has not helped them to bring forth and develop their own ideas. Indeed, Mairena is only too correct, for we gradually become aware of the partial failure of his pedagogical method. At the beginning of the book, there is at least some effort to employ meaningful dialogue. Even a character or two begin to emerge, especially the class auditor. When Mairena evokes a dialogue, however, he tends to make sport of the students; there are very few examples of his leading the student through dialogue to the triumph of discovering knowledge or insight. Little by little, Mairena begins to expound at greater length and almost without interruption, and the repeated phrase, "Mairena is speaking to his students," becomes only a formula. Moreover, occasionally Mairena is projected as talking with his cronies in the street, having deserted his seminar entirely. This is a reflection of that great gulf that still exists in Spain between professor and students; in practice he obviously cannot take his students seriously. Toward the end of the book, he is merely making speeches in his own ironic and low-keyed manner.

In his examination of conscience, Mairena thus becomes aware (as do we) that he has fallen into the trap of almost total self-concentration upon his own concerns, even while preaching "otherness," especially the aspect of brotherhood. He undoubtedly realizes that he has used clever logic to attack the idea of "masses" by asking, How can we add up individuals? Yet he understands that in his self-concern even with his class of interested individuals he has turned them into "masses" by haranguing them as an undifferentiated group. In a general sense, Mairena must realize that his failure adequately to reach the individuals of his class has extensive applications. In regard to the book *Juan de Mairena*, probably the more it becomes short general essays, without the personal interchanges between professor and students who are characters, the less it becomes a work of art. Moreover, Mairena's ambitious plans for a Popular School of Superior Wisdom cannot hope to become *popular* or of the people if he cannot or will not reach them. If he cannot develop this one School, he cannot hope to see his schools spread so as to influence the destiny of all Spain, and of course influencing the destiny of Spain has been his goal. Thus Mairena, rightly or wrongly, feels a sense of failure because he has gone too much his own way. As we have seen earlier, Machado expressed just such a failure in *Fields of Castile*, and even Unamuno in an examination of conscience admitted that he too had in a critical time "done only his own thing," as we put it nowadays.

III   *Machado's Prose Style*

In his creation of *Juan de Mairena* and his philosophical spec-ulations, Machado achieved an impressive example of prose style, a style he had been consciously perfecting in his earlier limited prose output. Given the fact of Mairena's modest back-ground in philosophy, his skepticism, and sardonic humor, Machado's style must reflect this type of character. Mairena him-self says style should be grounded upon two maxims: First, in order to speak and write well, one should choose essential themes; and, second, if one has a naturally clear style, why try to improve it toward obscurity? Machado was accustomed to much dry didacticism, windy rhetoric, and obscurity in Spanish writing; surely from his French studies he was impressed by the clarity and elegance of the best French prose. In *Juan de Mairena* he pointed his style toward the spoken language, as in fine dialogue, with a careful progression from one idea to anoth-er, and with coherence in the different sections. While basically his phrasing is typical of formal prose style, Machado's particular element of style is the injection of folk elements as a contrast. Mairena's ordinary background and his keen interest in popular wisdom make these descents in tone believable and effective. He attacks pedantry at every turn. For example, he approves a student's translation of "The consuetudinary events which come to pass in the boulevard" as "What happens in the street." In a most learned discussion he will say, "Kant wasn't sucking his thumb when he said . . ." At the other extreme, Mairena is not afraid of parading his learning on occasion, with phrases and ideas in Latin, French, or English. But the moment he is ap-proaching pedantry, he lowers the tone with a humorous or an ironic phrase. Every paragraph in *Juan de Mairena*, no matter how brief, gives the effect of being carefully thought out and expressed with clarity and grace.

IV   *Conclusion*

The *Juan de Mairena* series, which at first suffered a confused critical reception, has gradually become accepted and has added significantly to Machado's stature as a literary figure in the

Generation of 98. The piecemeal publication of the series during the confusion just before and during the Civil War of 1936-39 undoubtedly detracted from its impact upon the reading public. Moreover, since at that time Machado was thought of primarily as the poet of *Fields of Castile*, many of his colleagues failed to understand his purpose in publishing the articles. Even twenty years later, the distinguished literary historian Valbuena Prat fails to mention the book in his three-volume *Historia de la literatura española*. But poet-critic Luis Cernuda has asserted that in *Juan de Mairena* Machado, "without anyone's realizing it, was making the sharpest commentary of the period," even including that of Ortega y Gasset.[24] This is patently an exaggeration, for as a formal essayist Ortega has no rival in his period. Cernuda's remark, however, has a grain of truth. The contemporary reader is likely to distrust Ortega's towering formal structures and to prefer the more modest "notes" of Machado. Certainly Machado's ability to make his comments pertinent and tightly focused is outstanding. This talent for concentration is Machado's strong point in an inevitable comparison with Unamuno. Unamuno was a great "commentator," author of countless articles initially begun from the stimulation of reading some other work. While all his articles have at least a few nuggets of stimulating commentary, Unamuno felt free to meander in whatever direction he chose, without much regard for the work or author with which he began. Therefore, while Unamuno's total contribution is undoubtedly superior to Machado's, Machado surpasses him in the cogency of his argumentation and his concentration on the live cultural issues. Machado's *Juan de Mairena*, in addition to being a successful literary work, is a vital document for understanding the period of the Generation of 98.

CHAPTER 6

The Experiment in Theater

IT was after arriving in Segovia in 1919 that Antonio Machado slowly but steadily forced himself out of his exile of brooding solitude and began to participate in cultural and political affairs. Apparently becoming dissatisfied with his image in the literary world as a prematurely old poet nursing a few memories, he began to experience a renewal of his physical and mental energies. While living in provincial Segovia, he fulfilled the monotonous duties of his teaching position during the week, but he developed the habit of spending weekends in Madrid, where his brother Manuel always provided a stimulating literary *tertulia*. Manuel knew most of the important cultural figures and all the literary gossip circulating in the capital. In the course of these discussions, apparently he conceived the idea of competing in the theater in Madrid.[1] Perhaps because this was a daring step for Antonio, he and Manuel (who had remained very close) decided together to begin by collaborating upon some adaptations of Spanish Golden Age plays. The brothers' biographer makes it clear, however, that the further idea of writing original plays was Antonio's, and that a reluctant Manuel was convinced by his younger brother's enthusiasm.[2]

As residents for many years in Madrid, both brothers had been interested in the theater. As we have mentioned earlier, Antonio enjoyed a very brief fling as an actor during his early manhood, and continued his friendship with the actor Ricardo Calvo. Manuel, in his early years, actually wrote four plays, two of them in collaboration with others (not Antonio), but apparently he was not encouraged to continue by their reception. Manuel's credentials as a critic were impressive. Beginning in 1915 he became drama critic for the important daily *El Liberal*, and in 1918 published a volume called *A Year of Theater*. It happened that in 1920 Manuel reviewed García Lorca's first play, a resounding failure which he, however, treated benevolently. Moreover, the fact that Manuel knew some influential theatrical producers undoubtedly proved to be a practical benefit.

The Machados began their collaboration by developing modern adaptations of some well-known Golden Age plays. At this point, Manuel's contribution must have been significant, because he had a position in the National Library with ready access to source materials. The brothers began with Tirso de Molina's *El condenado por desconfiado*, important in the seventeenth century for its theological theme. Premiered in January, 1924, this adaptation of Tirso de Molina proved to be quite successful, provoking not only favorable critical comment, but also stimulating further discussion of the theological ideas of the original drama. Two plays of Lope de Vega were also adapted and staged, *Hay verdades que en amor* in 1925 and *La niña de plata* the next year. In these adaptations the Machados compressed, deleted, and shifted scenes, and of course had to work their revisions while retaining the verse forms in which these plays were written.[3]

I   *The Problem of Collaboration*

Since in this book we are of course attempting to explicate the life and work of Antonio Machado, we find it pertinent, before beginning a discussion of the Machados' original plays, to bring up the question of the relative contribution of each to the plays they wrote. The brothers themselves could easily have explained their methods, but when asked, each, in what passed for modesty, preferred to give major credit to the other. We suggest that perhaps there was a deeper reason. In general, later critics have not attempted to discuss the relative contribution of each brother, except for some of the most obvious and superficial features. Since in recent years Antonio's reputation as a profound poet and thinker has grown while Manuel's has diminished, there has been a tendency to give Antonio credit for the more important ideas, and Manuel for more superficial aspects, above all those of form and the Andalusian themes. Few critics have positively declared one brother's contribution to be superior to the other's. In a notable exception, Valbuena Prat, a major historian of the Spanish theater, has written recently that the Machados' theater shows the hand of Manuel in "tone, manner, and substance."[4] We are convinced of the opposite: that the themes and characters of the Machados' theater are essentially Antonio's, while Manuel served importantly in shaping the form of the plays.

That the relative contribution of each brother was unequal is suggested by later evidence. When the Machados' brother Joaquín was questioned on this matter, he declared that the biographer Pérez Ferrero, who suggested an approximately equal contribution, was "off the track" and added significantly: "We who know exactly don't consider it discreet to reveal it."[5] Joaquín's word *discreet* is surprising, because out of brotherly loyalty alone he could have avoided an answer. Since the only indiscreet thing in either brother's life was perhaps Antonio's experience with Guiomar, is Joaquín suggesting that the plays are connected with her? (Later in the letter from which we are quoting, he specifically refuses to discuss Guiomar.)

In the creation of dramatic works, it is axiomatic that the playwright should experience an inner necessity to project himself into characters and actions which express his own feelings, albeit indirectly. When we consider this for the Machados, it is clear that in the 1920's Antonio's creative energies were again at zenith, while Manuel's had been faltering for a number of years. In that period, as some of his poetry indicates, Antonio's vital energies began to revive, and he began to project himself outward into political and cultural activity, such as his work on the adaptations. Then around 1926, he met Guiomar, who (as we have previously discussed) is intimately connected with a crisis in his life and work. We know specifically that Antonio recast the theme of the brothers' most successful play so that Guiomar became a model for the heroine (this to be discussed later). Given this fact, it is not difficult to interpret most of their plays as Antonio's psychological projections of his difficult relationship with Guiomar. Such an interpretation of course does not affect the critical value of the plays. Further evidence of Antonio's necessity to dramatize himself is found in his insistent creation of *personae.* During these years he created Abel Martín, a poet keenly interested in love, and Juan de Mairena, both of whom express a specific aspect of Antonio's nature.

In contrast to Antonio, Manuel was even apathetic toward creative work (especially poetry) during this whole decade. After producing promising books in the *modernista* manner earlier in the century, in 1921 Manuel published a very brief volume significantly entitled *Ars moriendi*, followed fourteen years later by an equally brief one entitled *Phoenix.* These titles indicate what was happening to his poetry. Pérez Ferrero apologetically traces this painful period in Manuel's life, but can find no reason for his apathy. Even his friends reproached him, but he insisted upon continuing only the somewhat superficial literary activity in which he had always participated. Certainly Manuel remained close to the theater as spectator and critic, thus preparing himself to help with the structure and form of plays.

In general, the critics who have commented briefly on the question of each brother's contribution have indicated as Manuel's the parts of the plays which have a strong Andalusian flavor, especially popular or folk elements. This seems important, for most of their plays have an Andalusian setting. It is true that in 1912 Manuel published his *Cante hondo*, which are poems of love, death, and fatalism in the Andalusian (or flamenco) manner. But Manuel was really a cosmopolitan poet like his idol Rubén Darío; he was not a poet close to the earth, and his poems of gypsy swagger often revealed a bit of pose. Antonio of course was born in Andalusia and learned its folklore from his father. While he began as a Symbolist and as the poet of Castile, in the 1920's he turned strongly to Andalusian folk poetry and folklore as distilled wisdom, even becoming a bit tiresome in his insistence upon the values therein. Although the folk elements in Manuel's writing are often labeled as superficial because of a certain surface gaiety, in fact, the genuine Andalusian manner is tragic and fatalistic, like the temperament of Antonio Machado. Thus again we suggest that the heart of the plays was Antonio's contribution, and we shall comment on specific instances in the discussion following.

II   *Background of the Theater*

As literary figures of importance, the Machados were stimulated to write theater by their awareness of a much-discussed decline of the Spanish stage in the twentieth century.[6] Both realized, however, since Manuel was especially close to the theater, that their immediate problem was to compete with the established dramatists. The great playwright Jacinto Benavente had dominated the theater during the whole period of the Generation of 98. Beginning just before the turn of the century, he continued to produce play after play of critical and financial success. An innovator who replaced the melodramatic José Echegaray, Spain's first Nobel Prize winner, Benavente, who became the second winner of the award, depicted in a realistic and satirical manner the aristocratic society of which he was a part. Moreover, he also had outstanding success with two rural tragedies, *La malquerida* and *Señora ama*, and a philosophical comedy, *Los intereses creados*. Above all, Benavente was a craftsman whose plays were always technically outstanding, but by 1925 many followers of his theater were disappointed with the continuing ordinariness, the trivial domestic details, of his social satire. While the Machados, as literary figures, were undoubtedly aware of his shortcomings, as budding playwrights they respected his critical and financial success, as their fervent dedication to him of their first play proves.

The leading figures of the Generation of 98 were especially concerned with the state of decline in the Spanish theater. They deplored the lack of profundity in the plays the theatergoing public preferred, and placed some of the blame upon the theatrical producers, who as businessmen were controlling the artistic quality of what could be produced on the stage. These literary figures, who owed their reputations to success with genres other than drama, had persistent hopes of renovating the theater. As a rule, however, they refused to observe the techniques necessary for successful drama. Unamuno wrote a dozen plays in his long career, all suffused with the intense conflicts characteristic of his work. Yet few of these dramas were even offered for stage production. Typical of them is *El hermano Juan, o el mundo es teatro*, in which he attempts to exploit the Don Juan theme. Although interesting to read as a reflection of Unamuno's personality, the characters and thematic development are not sufficiently objective to allow the work to stand as theater. Ramón del Valle-Inclán wrote a trilogy of novels in dialogue form which he called *Comedias bárbaras*, in which his grandiose theme is the development of the archetypal family (in the Jungian sense). Some of his later works in his *esperpento* manner (a stylized deformation of reality) are powerfully dramatic, but unsuitable as conventional theater.

Of importance in this period is Jacinto Grau, a contemporary (though not considered a member) of the Generation of 98. Grau has remained something of an anomaly in the Spanish theater. Like most of the literary figures, he inveighed against the condition of stagnation in the theater. Somewhat like Valle-Inclán, he attempted to create better plays by developing themes involving myth and Spanish traditions. Typical is *El burlador que no se burla*, his particular projection of the Don Juan theme. Moreover, Grau was potentially the outstanding Vanguard playwright in the 1920's in Spain. His *El señor de Pigmalión*, written in 1921, is something like Pirandello's famous *Six Characters in Search of an Author* and Capek's *R. U. R.*, for in all three the problem of reality and artistic creation is treated in a novel way. Although Grau's play was successful in Paris and he earned an international reputation, he failed to impress the conservative theatergoing public in Madrid. Since his approach was intellectual and his form a lucid prose, his plays now read well for their ideas, but in general they suffer from an unconventional structure and a lack of human emotion.

Although Benavente had finally established prose dialogue as the basic form in the Spanish theater, many literary figures, who were often also poets, continued to strive to produce what is generally called "poetic theater." The proponents of poetic theater usually, though not always, preferred to write in poetic form, but above all, they insisted on poetic treatment of profound or universal themes, with a certain elevation of tone and sentiment beyond the normal fare of commercial theater. Outstanding examples of poetic theater have been rare. Perhaps the most enduring success before the Machados' appearance was Marquina's *En Flandes se ha puesto el sol*, a play of historical theme which extols Spain's influence in the Low Countries. Marquina's *Don Luis Mejía*, another treatment of the Don Juan theme from the point of view of his antagonist, also achieved a certain popularity. The creation of successful poetic theater was hardly more than a dream of the literary group until García Lorca appeared, and even he produced a limited number of examples.

III   *The Major Plays of the Machados*

When the Machados embarked upon their career as dramatists, by temperament and experience as poets, they were committed to poetic drama, but they were determined also to produce successful plays for the commercial theater in Madrid. Apparently since their adaptation of Tirso de Molina was a success, they modeled their first original play fairly closely after the formula used by the Golden Age dramatists. The tragicomedy *Desdichas de la fortuna, o Julianillo Valcárcel* (*The Workings of Fate, or Julianillo Valcárcel*) was premiered on February 9, 1926, in the Princesa in Madrid.

For their theme, the Machados returned to the seventeenth century and the political maneuvering of the Count-Duke of Olivares. The Count-Duke at the opening of the play has just brought to the court his bastard son Julianillo Valcárcel, who had been enjoying a fantastic life of picaresque and soldierly adventures in the Indies. Julianillo is being groomed as the Count-Duke's successor. Julianillo outspokenly refuses to participate in the artificial life of the court and continues to cultivate friends of a low social level. He refuses to separate himself from Leonor, a woman of common birth whom he deeply loves, but the Count-Duke finally forces him to marry Doña Juana, the Count-Duke's cousin. Under pressure then to follow the court life in the palace, Julianillo loses his will to live, pines away into illness, and finally dies, still imprisoned by the memory of Leonor.

The Workings of Fate, according to a witness at the première, was a "complete success,"[7] and the few critics who have discussed the play have continued to praise the Machados' initial effort. Since the premiere was connected with a political celebration not related to the play, however, we cannot be sure of the quantity of its actual impact. As the subject matter is historical, coinciding with the typical Golden Age play, there are certain stylized scenes which could be projected: the court scene, the tavern scene (a sketch of "low life"), the love scene, etc. Perhaps because of the formality and stylization of these scenes, the Machados were able to use their talents in creating poetic dialogue of very convincing quality. Both poets, experienced in handling the popular octosyllable used basically in the dialogue, were able to sustain brisk movement when it was called for, and to achieve a heightened lyrical quality in more intense moments. Moreover, the cast of characters is developed with a completeness perhaps not to be expected in a first play. Even Gil Blas, a lieutenant of the Count-Duke, comes over as a real character.

But as a modern play written in the twentieth century, *The Workings of Fate* suffers a serious shortcoming. Critics have tended to call it "classical" or "traditional," meaning that it is imitative of the drama of the Golden Age, of Lope de Vega and Calderón. This defense of traditionality was actually basic in the Machados' ideas concerning the theater. In a short manifesto published at the end of their dramatic career, they began by declaring that "The theater is an art of tradition," and that "no important work has been produced without the collaboration of the centuries."[8] Apparently the Machados were upholding tradition because they objected to the emphasis upon the trivial and the "domestic" in many commercial plays of their day. But it is doubtful that they set out to write an imitation of a Golden Age play; they must have intended to develop elements of their own, of pertinence to their modern audience. Their failure to develop and present their own theme effectively is the shortcoming of the play. In *The Workings of Fate*, the first three acts seem imitative of a Golden Age play, while in the fourth act (this addition of a fourth act violated Golden Age practice), apparently they are trying to project modern subjectivism. Dr. Valbuena finds this part of the play "typically *modernista*, because of the fading and melancholy love."[9] Another critic passionately declares the play successful because of this theme: "Julián dies of love, and for love, which is of all things the most beautiful."[10] This all-consuming type of love is indeed the Machados' theme, but in part they fail with the character who represents it. Julianillo, a traditionally heroic, individualistic character, is not developed in dramatic context, and the whole last act itself seems to dribble away on the stage. This inability to terminate a play with a strong last act became somewhat chronic with the Machados.

For the beginning of the next season of the theater in the spring of 1927, the Machados presented *Juan de Mañara*, based on the legend of a notorious seventeenth-century libertine who finally repented and became a saint. Mañara is one of the figures who provided material for the elaboration of the Don Juan legend. The Machados thus joined a large group of their genera-tion—Unamuno, Valle-Inclán, Azorín, Grau, Martínez Sierra, Marquina, etc.—who seized upon and treated each in his own fashion the Don Juan theme as handed down from Tirso de Molina and José Zorrilla. Although this theme is historical, in their second play we see Antonio's personality beginning to assert itself, for the essence of *Juan de Mañara* is its moral or ethical theme. Let us recall again that Manuel's poetry, in the *modernista* manner, was permanently aesthetic. Antonio very early had shifted from the aesthetic to the moral: we recall that in his famous "Portrait" he dared to say he was "good." In his philosophical writings he emphasized the idea that, despite pre-vailing tendencies of his age, he was always bound by moral and ethical considerations. Moreover, the Don Juan theme continued to interest him seriously. In *Juan de Mairena* he concludes a brief but stimulating discussion with some of his particular ideas. "In a truce with the Eros of procreation, Don Juan doesn't re-nounce the flesh, but like the monk renounces engendering in it. When he repents, he becomes a friar—in a way he already was."[11] Here, in addition to another example of Antonio's preoccupation with procreation, is a sketch of the Don Juan of *Juan de Mañara*.

The Machados' Don Juan, from a titled Andalusian family noted for its extremes of conduct in the past, is a character of the contemporary period given to extravagant living. Before the play opens, he has seduced Elvira and carried her off to Paris, an experience which leads to her moral collapse. Now back in Seville, Don Juan continues his amatory success by rapidly con-quering the heart of Beatriz, who was destined for the convent, Becoming involved again with Elvira when she shoots to death the husband she has married for his money, Don Juan helps her to escape to Paris. Meanwhile Beatriz, now aggressively in love with Don Juan, pursues him to Paris. As the third and last act opens, Juan, back in Seville, has married Beatriz from a sense of duty, but unable to make amends for having destroyed Elvira's soul, he has converted himself into a saint, and goes about spreading charity in the town. Both women try to save him, Beatriz for a normal human life as her husband, Elvira as an act of charity, but he soon dissipates his strength in the severity of his religious life and dies in an aura of saintliness.

Juan de Mañara is the Machados' attempt, against difficult odds in our century, to create a convincing drama on the theme of the essential importance of the ethical values of man. In the play Don Juan rapidly becomes, not the seducer of many as is traditional, but a moral being concerned with love and responsibility toward two women. The important thematic moment occurs when he looks into Elvira's soul and sees himself: "I have looked into my soul / In the light of another conscience / And seen that mine was turbid" (III, iii). Evil, which is unconcern or perhaps hatred for others, rules much of human destiny; human life is the struggle against that evil. Juan becomes spiritually separated from Beatriz for a subtle reason. Originally destined for the convent and a life of love for all mankind, Beatriz, when she falls in love with him, discovers that she actually prefers the "selfish" love of Don Juan alone, and a normal life of domesticity. In fact, she fights aggressively and finally wins him legally. But Don Juan feels a greater responsibility toward Elvira, and dedicates himself so fiercely to Christian charity that he sacrifices his life itself.

This drastic solution proves to be somewhat ineffective as drama, for a number of reasons. In the Golden Age such total changes from sinner to saint occurred historically and were therefore believable in the theater, but even in conservative Spain a skeptical modern audience would need to be convinced by the dramatic action itself. The Machados apparently lacked the dramatic resources for this difficult task. In the first two acts, Don Juan is entirely convincing as a character, but his conversion occurs *between* the second and the third acts, so that the third seems more like an epilogue to the first two. Don Juan, like Julianillo of *The Workings of Fate*, tends to collapse as a character in Act III. It is unfortunate that this partial failure at the conclusion should mar an otherwise interesting play with effective dialogue and even some well-developed secondary characters.

In 1928, the Machados, perhaps suspecting that their first two plays were too traditional, made a change of direction with an entirely modern piece called *Las adelfas* (*Bitter Oleander*). In spite of certain touches of romanticism and a typical Andalusian scene, the play is not largely Manuel's as one critic has suggested;[12] the awareness of Freud and the attempt to develop "Freudian" dialogue in the play indicates a major concern of Antonio's. In *Juan de Mairena*[13] Antonio reveals a keen interest in developing a new kind of dialogue to express the voice of the subconscious in the theater. Mairena even confesses to have written a Freudian drama of massive proportions and great novelty called *The Grand Climax*. Moreover, there is, especially in this play, a consistent sprinkling of ideas which we recognize as Antonio's because of their presence in his other prose work. Finally, though this is conjectural, within the play itself (II, iv) there is a tiny psychological "play within the play" which sounds suspiciously like a projection of the Antonio-Guiomar relationship.

In the plot, Araceli, the widowed young Duchess of Tormes, sets out to analyze and evaluate her relations with Alberto, her deceased husband, who had recently died in what was either an accident or a suicide. To understand herself, Araceli consults with her doctor, Carlos Montes, who was Alberto's best friend and who also suffered an unrequited love for Araceli. There is also Rosalía, formerly Araceli's friend but also Alberto's lover. Into this already complicated situation enters Salvador Montoya, a supremely confident, self-made modern capitalist, who was formerly Rosalía's lover. After all these characters have an opportunity to bare their motives and pursue their respective goals, Salvador ultimately wins Araceli's hand, thereby (as his name implies) saving her from a wasted life of meaningless guilt and isolation from the mainstream of life.

The excessive complication of the plot should not obscure the fact that *Bitter Oleander* is a modern psychological drama of definite value. In an early passage of the dialogue we learn that

the authors (and especially Antonio) are aware of the new
Freudian psychology, and the characters proceed to reveal both
the good and the evil in themselves. Not even the deceased
Alberto is spared this searching analysis of weaknesses. The
Machados were to say later in their manifesto that the contemporary dramatist now has to be aware of two kinds of dialogue,
the Socratic and the Freudian. The first presents man as a being
of reason; the second, exploring the subconscious, attempts to
touch upon deep truths sometimes unknown to the subject himself. Of course the Machados had no exact technical knowledge
of modern psychology, but their awareness of Freud indicates
that they were willing to explore all the darker facets of human
character, even if the results were disturbing.

In this drama, in addition, there is development of a social
theme which later became insistent in Antonio's prose work. He
attacks the class usually identified by the *señorito*, the bright
but frivolous young man of fine family who is an unproductive
member of his society. Antonio contrasts him unfavorably with
the figure of the modern executive, the man of energy, talent
and decision—this latter quality to be admired above all, since
Antonio himself lacked it. Salvador Montoya of course represents this new man. In developing Montoya's actions, however,
the Machados fall into the most serious fault of the play. In the
first two acts, in the brisk and incisive dialogue, we are convinced of the seriousness of the play. But in the last act, when
the heroic Salvador arrives almost miraculously to save Araceli
on the night of St. John in a romantic Andalusian setting, the
play almost becomes just another romantic comedy.

Even with this happy ending, however, *Bitter Oleander* was
only mildly successful in Madrid, enjoying a very short run. For
the Machados, this setback in their first attempt with modern
psychological drama was probably unfortunate, because even
though the play in many ways shows outstanding promise, they
must have been discouraged from beginning another play in
this manner.

In 1929, the Machados achieved their most enduring dramatic
success in Madrid working with a traditional theme of the Andalusian *cante jondo* (the deep song) in *La Lola se va a los puertos*
(*La Lola Goes off to Sea*), premiered at the Fontalba Theater

with the actress Lola Membrives. In fact, Lola, who had starred in one of the Machados' adaptations, was largely responsible for their composition of the play. Of course neither brother needed much urging to work with an Andalusian folk theme. The Machados set out to rework a traditional situation: the older Andalusian landowner of noble background competes with his own son for the affections of a lass, often of the lower class, but who possesses beauty and charm. In this plot Don Diego becomes fascinated by Lola, a girl of gypsy origins, who is an outstanding *cantaora*, or singer of the *cante jondo*. His son, José Luis, is also charmed by Lola, but he is also being pursued by Rosario, who is of his own class. To this standard plot the Machados added Rafael Heredia, a great flamenco guitarist, who serves as Lola's accompanist. During the play all three men succumb to Lola's charm and want to marry her, but she kindly but firmly puts each in his own place: Don Diego returns to society, now given to charitable works, José Luis is to marry Rosario, and Heredia continues in his role as only the guitarist for Lola. She chooses to continue to be the essence, or the symbol, of the *cante jondo*.

In this drama, whose substance is mostly Antonio's, the theme is not the usual Andalusian (and universal) one in which the artist discovers life through love; here the artist (La Lola), who shows the way of life to others, must by her destiny lose herself in sublimation, becoming a symbol of her art, the song of the *cante jondo*. Antonio himself clarified this theme in a letter to Guiomar. Before he met Guiomar, the brothers had already begun a play of typical Andalusian theme; then, under her spell, Antonio confessed that he recast the part of La Lola, making her more idealized and ultimately a symbol.[14] Actually, Antonio clearly preferred life over art, but the unattainability of Guiomar forced him in this instance to choose art. This accounts for the fact that, although called a comedy, Lola's choosing to remain a symbol of the *cante jondo* seems like a sacrifice with overtones of tragedy. Actually, she has no clear reasons of either head or heart for rejecting Rafael's love, and both she and Rafael seem headed toward a life of "dream," the state of illusion which Antonio Machado thought life always works out to be.

The Machados achieved an example of competent poetic theater in *La Lola*. The success of the play depends largely upon the depth of the two main characters, La Lola and the guitarist Heredia, whose voice is often that of the poet and philosopher Antonio Machado himself. Antonio set out to make La Lola intensely human—aware of her own worth, compassionate, of elevated spirit. And we are not merely told of these qualities; Lola demonstrates them in the dramatic action of the play, although in the last part she begins perhaps to become a bit too ethereal and detached. Her role demands a great actress (such as was Lola Membrives), with special subtlety in handling dialogue of great density. The character of Rafael Heredia gradually becomes more profound as the play progresses, for it is in the density of his dialogue where the philosopher Antonio Machado himself often speaks. As poets, the Machados were probably guilty of prolonging important speeches and overloading them with lyrically expressed ideas, whereas a craftsman like Benavente would spread his ideas more thinly in the interchange of dialogue, so that the audience could more easily assimilate them. Apparently from experience, the Machados recognized that Spanish actors too often depended upon bombastic delivery, for in their manifesto they called for a renovation of the normal acting manner involving a concentration upon the meaning of lines and a deeper penetration into the subtleties of the role. The poetic dialogue in the Machados' usual manner is especially demanding of the actors, but it is the correct vehicle for the stylized theme of *La Lola*.

After the success of *La Lola* in 1929, the Machados found themselves with a reputation to sustain, but apparently their inspiration was beginning to fade. They began a new play called *La prima Fernanda* (*Cousin Fernanda*) in 1930; however, after their finishing two acts, Antonio confessed in a private letter to Guiomar that they were struggling with a third act, not with effective dramatic construction, but with a convincing conclusion itself.[15] Finally premiered in 1931, *Cousin Fernanda* is a comedy of modern setting in the world of high finance and upper-level political decision. Cousin Fernanda is a young widow, who had been married to a rich Polish prince. Now back in Spain, she is pursued by the politician Corbacho and the financier Leonardo, although the latter's wife Matilde is a friend of Fernanda's. Both men want Fernanda, but neither will ultimately surrender his dedication to his work. Therefore, Fernanda, who is seeking an all-consuming love, rearranges all the lives around her as they were before her arrival, and, as the play ends, prepares to depart for Warsaw.

Cousin Fernanda is an effective comedy in the tradition of the *alta comedia* in Spain. After writing a number of plays, the Machados' technical ability manifests itself clearly. The scenes move briskly and naturally; in general the characters begin properly to emerge from their speech and actions. The difficult triangle between Fernanda, Leonardo, and his wife is handled with naturalness and some psychological penetration, especially in the first two acts. The political satire, handled almost as farce, is somewhat effective, though mild by present-day standards. On the negative side, perhaps the verse form is a mistake, because the materials are clearly prosaic. Moreover, the insistent "modernity" in the play, seen in the breezy dialogue about sports, automobiles, etc., seems at times forced. The central theme of the play is the power of all-consuming love, but a shadow of artificiality surrounds Fernanda and robs the play of a certain amount of seriousness. All in all, however, the play is a fast-moving, modern comedy which should have been a popular success at least. Surprisingly it was not, because it apparently became entangled in the heated politics of the day.

For their last major play—in the spring of 1932—the Machados staged *La duquesa de Benamejí* (*The Duchess of Benamejí*). The entire circumstances surrounding this play are puzzling. It was a time of intense political activity and turmoil. Antonio personally, apparently becoming disillusioned with the Guiomar affair, was in the process of forsaking poetry for philosophical prose. In spite of the increasing seriousness of the atmosphere, however, the play is fantastically romantic in the nineteenth-century manner.

In the plot, the young Duchess, loved by the young lieutenant Carlos of her class, falls in love with Lorenzo, a Robin Hood type of bandit of common origins, whom Carlos is trying to capture. Lorenzo is also loved by Rocío, a beautiful gypsy girl. Both young ladies take to the mountains in pursuit of the dashing Lorenzo, and the Duchess briefly enjoys his love. Through a trick, Carlos captures Lorenzo, and when the Duchess tries to help him escape and flee with him, Rocío stabs her fatally. Lorenzo, now losing all desire to live, refuses to escape and surrenders himself to be shot.

Given this extravagant plot, which has all the elements Antonio preached against (above all the "tourist" view of Andalusia), what is the point of this play? Since there are elements of Romanticism in some of their earlier plays, no critic has set *The Duchess of Benamejí* apart as revealing a different intent on the part of the playwrights. It could easily be read as a satire against certain Romantic plays of the nineteenth century, but the Machados had no particular dislike of such plays. We find it difficult to believe that Antonio would spend his talent on an extravagantly romantic play when the political situation and his own personal life were in a desperate condition. Therefore, when we consider that Antonio's work was becoming increasingly skeptical and ironical (and even a "little cynical," he said) in this period, we suspect that in this play's melodramatic glorification of love we have Antonio's bitter-sweet and final ironic commentary on his unrequited love for Guiomar. The central idea in *The Duchess of Benamejí* concerns the Duchess' desertion of class and responsibilities for an all-consuming passion. Machado later repeated this idea of a Duchess deserting her class for love in a snatch of dialogue in *Juan de Mairena*, also in a situation of irony.[16] Although Guiomar never quite deserted her class and responsibilities, the fact that the possibility existed until about the time of this play provided Antonio with an ironic and desperate situation. Probably he also enjoyed the further irony that the play, in the construction of scenes, the development of characters, and in the poetry of the important dialogues, turned out to be one of the brothers' best efforts.

One other commendable effort of the Machados, which departs somewhat from their regular manner and choice of theme, is *El hombre que murió en la guerra* (*The Man Who Died in the War*), surprisingly prophetic considering the date of composition of the first draft. Largely unknown before Antonio's death, the play was made public by Manuel, who daringly (given the liberal political theme) had it produced in Madrid in 1941, not long after the Civil War. At that time Manuel insisted that it was written around 1928, but all the internal evidence suggests that Antonio must have reworked it later, around 1934. Of all their plays, surely this one is in essence Antonio's, for it is filled with the liberal and even radical political ideas he continued to develop until his death, while Manuel gradually became staunchly conservative. Additional evidence of Antonio's guiding hand are the many specific ideas also appearing in his other work, especially *Juan de Mairena*. *The Man Who Died in the War* is the Machados' only play in prose, the correct vehicle for the ideas it contains. In the protagonist's search for identity, we see also the Machados' interest in the Vanguard Italian dramatist Pirandello.

At the beginning of *The Man Who Died in the War*, the aristocratic family of Don Andrés de Zúñiga is observing the tenth anniversary of the death of his son Juan, actually a bastard son who grew up with his mother. Suddenly there appears a man calling himself Miguel de la Cruz, who claims he was an intimate companion of Juan at the time of his death in World War I in France in 1918. Little by little Don Andrés and Guadalupe, Juan's childhood sweetheart, come to the realization that Miguel is actually Juan. At the conclusion Juan insists on leaving, but the possibility is left open for him to return "home," perhaps even to marry Guadalupe, with the implication that the family must accept him as a "new man," since the old type of man "died in the war."

This new man was the Machados' (and in this case almost completely Antonio's) vision of the ideal man of the epoch—young, liberal, intelligent, aggressive, suspicious of the past, and determined to create a new world. Juan is still a surprisingly contemporary character for us. He firmly believes that "There is something absurd in all wars." He insists that the privileged aristocratic family has to go, but not to be replaced by mass democracy. His belief is in the aristocracy of talent, where a man's first achievement is to be himself. According to Juan (voicing one of Antonio's specific ideas), should Jesus come again he would preach, not humility, but pride to the humble (III, viii). This new man also seeks a new woman, a woman who is first of all an individual who is developing her intellectual capacity, not just her domestic talents. Above all this new man of utter sincerity will be totally devoted to work, to the challenging task of making the great society a reality.

As a finished script for the theater, *The Man Who Died in the War* lacks sufficient development of the action of the characters in relation to the ideas they propound. This is understandable when we realize that apparently Manuel declined to work further on the play after Antonio's death. The main character is too much given to projecting and defending his ideas; the play was perhaps conceived initially too much as a set of ideas rather than as the action which good drama must be. As a document of this period, however, the play is a penetrating and visionary moment of inspiration for Spain, like much of *Juan de Mairena.* When it was finally staged by the Machados' old friend Ricardo Calvo after the Civil War, surely the intellectuals must have been bitterly aware that in the War this visionary Juan died and remained dead.

IV   *Conclusion*

In summary, the Machados achieved a moderate success in their attempts to create poetic theater, leaving at least two dramas of permanent value in Spanish literature, and three which have some commendable qualities. *La Lola Goes Off to Sea*, with proper staging to preserve the seriousness of the theme and fine actors in the main roles, can still be an effective play. As a modern psychological drama, *Bitter Oleander* is an adequate representative of the 1920's, in spite of its facile conclusion. *Julianillo Valcárcel* is an example among many of the Spanish playwrights' attempts to recreate Spain's glorious past and make it pertinent to the present. *Juan de Mañara* becomes a worthy example of what is almost a cycle of Don Juan plays in the modern period. *Cousin Fernanda*, an attractive, light modern comedy, reflects the important topical interests of the day. As would be expected, the Machados' greatest strength was in their creation of poetic dialogue. They modernized somewhat the traditional octosyllabic stanzas by employing more run-on lines to make the dialogue flow more naturally. As poets, however, they were sometimes guilty of prolonging speeches with lyric content, placing a strain upon both actor and audience.

In general, the Machados strove to meet the demands of the commercial theater, so that whatever problems they encountered in producing enduring poetic drama probably involve the personality of the Machados themselves, especially Antonio's. The critics of their theater have pointed out their persistent problem in writing a third or final act, without attempting to pursue the underlying reasons. We have assumed that the themes and characters of their plays came largely from Antonio, and certainly there is a consistency in them in that the main character is often a dominant, elevated, or unapproachable female figure—Leonor, Lola, Fernanda, Araceli. And the insistent central theme is the power of all-consuming love. Now in the early acts of their plays, these characters and themes are presented in a real world. There are many persuasive and memorable scenes with believable people, with real problems and passions. The promise of authentic love, however, clashes with a firm conviction of the skeptic Antonio that "All love is phantasy," and that even our existence is "apocryphal." The real and all-consuming love therefore had no possible function, making it difficult for the characters to resolve their situations convincingly. Since Antonio believed only in phantasy or illusion (for that matter, so did Manuel), the dramatic solutions often seemed extreme. At times they offered an extravagant romantic solution (as in *Bitter Oleander*), or the unconvincing demise of a main character (as in *Juan de Mañara*). Of course illusion (or evasion) as opposed to reality is entirely possible in the theater, and later the respected playwright Alejandro Casona created a corpus of drama suspended delicately between the illusory and the real worlds. But the Machados insisted on presenting a real world in the early acts, so that when later their protagonists drifted into illusion, they never quite discovered how to provide a convincing transition between the two worlds. In a sense Antonio is only repeating the general pattern of his poetry: after an engagement with the real world, he tends to drift into a world of *sueño* or illusion. This pattern, as we have pointed out before, is a typical one with the major figures of the Generation of 98.

CHAPTER 7

Machado's Position and Influence

A NTONIO MACHADO's permanent position in Spanish literature will depend largely upon his poetry and the unique human voice projected therein. At the same time, his *Juan de Mairena*, as the condensed expression of his personal, cultural, and philosophical speculations, has gradually become one of the important documents of Machado's generation. His drama, which offers the complexity of being a joint effort with his brother Manuel, will apparently retain a minor historical value, serving mainly for the light it casts on the development of Antonio's personality. As a poet, his place seems assured: there is general agreement in Spain that the giants of twentieth-century Spanish poetry are Miguel de Unamuno, Juan Ramón Jiménez, and Antonio Machado, with the probable inclusion of Federico García Lorca as a fourth. Outside Spain, Lorca, known both as a poet and dramatist, certainly enjoys a greater reputation than either Jiménez or Machado.

While Machado was given to modesty, Jiménez himself late in life declared (in a statement we have quoted before) that "Machado and I initiated the innermost voice (*lo interior*) in modern Spanish poetry," and added that Unamuno reintroduced the metaphysical themes.[1] By these words, Jiménez means that he and Machado were responsible for a renewal of Spanish poetry, with a strong assist from Unamuno. Such a renewal presupposes a previous state of decline; and it is certain that when Machado and Jiménez appeared on the scene Spanish poetry was at a low ebb. Previously important poets, such as Campoamor, Zorrilla, and Nuñez de Arce were no longer exerting influence. From Bécquer, who died prematurely, Machado developed his belief in the importance of poetry and a form in which to express his emotions. From Rubén Darío he also learned much of form and the need for intense dedication to both the spirit and craft of poetry.

Machado's progression and achievement as a poet he himself began to analyze in later years. In a rare moment of immodesty, he once jotted down a brief outline for the study of Spanish lyric poetry, giving special emphasis to a one-word analysis of the important poets of his period, including Darío, Jiménez, and his brother Manuel. He classified himself as a poet of *intimismo*, that is, of the innermost voice of consciousness.[2] In the Prologue of *Solitudes,* he called it a "deep palpitation of the spirit," a state of consciousness during which the poet sought to discover a few "true words." Machado thought of his *intimismo* in contrast with the early Jiménez' aesthetic Impressionism and with the early Darío's Modernism, characterized by excessive emphasis upon the external aspects of form. But by *intimismo* he was in no way suggesting the stripping away of reticence and propriety. In fact, Machado prided himself upon the fact that *Solitudes* was the first book of Spanish poetry in which even the anecdotal was proscribed.[3] His understanding of intimate can be meaningfully compared with that of our own Emily Dickinson.

Antonio Machado's *intimismo* gradually dissolved itself into his insistent projection of himself as a *poeta en el tiempo*, a poet of temporality in the full modern sense of the phrase. In the *Apocryphal Songbook* and in *Juan de Mairena*, he repeatedly enunciated his definition of the temporal, urging the reader to be aware that he was adding a modern dimension to what has been one of the common themes in poetry. Early he reached the intuition that his soul (or consciousness), absolutely solitary and unique, was immersed in its own time. He insistently called this "the essential heterogeneity of being." In this solitary state, however, he felt that his soul suffered an incurable yearning or nostalgia toward "otherness," the principal representatives of otherness being woman, his fellow man, and God. The poet's task was to sing this "vital time with its own vibration."[4] As Machado expressed it poetically, there is no "way" to follow; each soul makes its own way. This seemingly simple phrase is actually a negation of the Christian idea that Christ is the "way." When a medieval Christian poet such as Jorge Manrique sang of the temporal way, he was referring to the temporal nature of the body only, for at the same time he believed firmly in the eternal nature of the soul. Machado simply lost this Christian faith (as did the other important figures of his Generation of 98); therefore the anguish in his poetry sprang, not from the sadness of losing earthly pleasures, but from the finality of losing everything. Ultimately Machado reached the position that the poet sings only because of the anguish of feeling his soul enmeshed in time, awaiting the ever-present threat which is death.

As a poet of marked temporality, Machado found a way of expressing the temporal by becoming a *poeta en sueños*, a poet of time and memory. This theme is omnipresent in every period of his poetry. For Machado, there was no present; as he finally synthesized it, "Today is always yet." The "always" is the poet's past experience, which he must explore, elaborate, re-create in order to "save" it, to preserve it in memory against annihilation. Time in the present is always being transferred to the process of memory, of reverie, of the "dream." The "yet" is the time stretching out before the poet, and as Antonio grew older, he tended to project his dream toward the future, to create a world as he would have liked it to be. Machado found the germ of this process in Bécquer and the Romantic poets, and we should add that in Machado's whole generation each individual developed his own peculiar manner of recreating reality in dream and memory.

Throughout his poetic career, Machado's work is characterized by an oscillation between subjectivism and a persistent reaching out toward otherness. In the first period of *Solitudes*, the poet turned inward to reach an awareness of consciousness; in the "galleries" of the soul he sought to "surprise" and create an intimate monologue. This period ended in dissatisfaction: on the one hand his intuition dissolved into the rational thought of philosophy; on the other, he lost faith in subjectivism. In the second period, that of *Fields of Castile*, the poet looked outward and discovered the Castilian theme—the people, landscape, and problems of Castile and Spain. He also found a simple human love and recognized in his *elogios* the literary efforts of his colleagues. Unfortunately, his looking outward was beset by tragedy, for his love was terminated by the death of his wife, and his hopes for a new Spain soon became unrealizable. Thus he was driven back again upon himself, and he turned to philosophy. But in his third period, beginning around 1926, he enjoyed a renascence and reached out again toward otherness. This otherness took the form of a profound autumn love at the human level and a continued search for the objective reality of God at the metaphysical. But this time the poet armed himself with a "poet's metaphysics" that precluded defeat, for in his ironic way he argued that "the beloved is impossible" and that "God is nothingness." In the untouchable well of his consciousness, however, he discovered and continued to emphasize that the poet's essential task was that of singing his own vital, unique experience, fully aware of this tragic human condition.

The form in which Machado clothed his poetry was distinct and consistent. In form he was always a traditional poet, employing established meters and rhymes. Since his preferences in form were established early in the century, not even the aggressive formlessness of the Surrealists could sway him in later years. After a few early attempts, he consciously rejected the superficial aspects of verse, sonorous meters, and ingenious rhymes. In fact, he insisted that his poetry was not to be declaimed or even read aloud. In most of his verse he employed the standard hendecasyllable (like our pentameter), often along with heptasyllables. Given his interest in popular poetry, he also utilized the simple octosyllable or ballad line, with the unobtrusive assonance of Spanish poetry. In later years he began to insist upon this "sparse rhyme," or assonance, and in his emphasis upon temporality even began to call for "temporal rhyme," that is, rhyme upon the tenses of the verb. At the same time, however, he attempted to revive the sonnet form as an apt vehicle to express human emotion. In all his poetry, while rejecting the superficial brilliance of the *modernista* poets, Machado worked as diligently as they in achieving a low-keyed tone of simplicity and clarity and under-stressed music. In Machado, a general simplicity (as we have seen, some of his poems are extremely difficult) in no sense implies carelessness. Even a severe critic like Jiménez praised him for the naturalness of his poetic form. His rhymes always seem inevitable, without any strain; his lines flow with a naturalness which reveals none of the care and effort he expended on the form. This is of course the mark of a poet: to be able to cast the rebellious and formless elements of language into the form of good poetry without any evidence of strain and manipulation.

While Machado thus demonstrated a mastery of form within his essential poems, throughout his career he evidenced a weakness in the organization of his books of poetry, and even in his prose. He was never a prolific or even a consistently inspired poet (as was Jiménez, for example); therefore the composition of his books usually covered a period of years, during the course of which his themes and manner tended to change somewhat. As we noted in passing, such a change occurred during the writing of *Solitudes*, creating a problem of organization he could never quite resolve, even though he had several opportunities with later editions of his *Complete Poems*. Moreover, the quality of his poems is quite uneven. While critics have largely ignored this point, they have proved its validity by returning again and again to a limited number of his outstanding poems, passing over the rest. Surely Machado recognized that some of his poems were of lesser value, but he must have felt that all he chose to preserve in his *Complete Poems* served to fill out the record of his total poetic experience.

As we attempted to demonstrate in the discussion of his poetry, while Machado produced poetry of fairly distinct manner and theme in three periods, there is nevertheless a strong underlying unity in all his work. He insistently concentrated upon the essential things of man's existence. Focusing upon his own consciousness, he developed a preoccupation with time and memory, which involved a deep necessity to live fully the experiences of human existence. To express these experiences, he utilized consistently a small group of basic symbols: the symbols of water (fountain, river, sea), the road, and others. As his life situation changed, he was able to adapt his old symbols to the new situation, with a certain continuity always evident. When we view with some perspective all his poetry, the figure of a poet begins to emerge who is all of a piece, and it is this figure that remains alive in Spanish literature and life. This figure is essentially a solitary wayfarer upon the earth, more and more feeling himself alien upon the planet, but at the same time anguishing over the brevity of human existence. In another age he would probably have been a Transcendentalist; but, appearing at a critical moment in the disintegration of his Catholic culture, he became an Existentialist against his will. Thus finding himself utterly isolated within the temporality of his own consciousness, Machado struggled to believe in the objective reality of the world, people, and especially God. And he never quite succeeded.

Machado's work was increasingly pervaded by a skepticism, a universal skepticism. His skepticism sprang from his sense of being in need, of realizing man's humble position in the universe. It sprang from his sense of dread, a dread of annihilation, an intuition traceable to Kierkegaard, and expressed in Spanish by Unamuno. Intensely aware of this human predicament (which has of course become the prevailing attitude of our time), he discovered two courses of action. First, he attempted to elevate poetry to an act of living, or *seeing*, which he declared to be above and beyond skepticism. And second, in his skeptic humor (found often in his prose), by smiling sadly at himself and his ideas he managed partly to free himself from the despair over the human condition. While Machado's skepticism thus suffused his whole being, his poetry itself he regarded as a *positive* creation of the spirit of man. His typical poem seems to be poised at the brink of despair, but in it he almost always achieved a certain noble control of himself, of his poetic form, and of a theme from which we can somehow draw strength. In later years Machado made his own a deep intuition of Dostoevski: that as Western man became more alienated from God, he would not revert to savagery, but in his great need would in fact turn even more strongly toward his fellow man for love and comfort. While Machado's position was skeptical, his personal faith unrealized, his record of expressed defeats persistent, he stubbornly retained a faith in the dignity of the spirit of man upon the earth, and his work has continued to be appreciated as an expression of that particular faith.

Antonio Machado's influence has continued to increase in the years after his death, and today he is a living personality in Spanish poetry and literature. From the time of the publication of *Solitudes* in 1907, he became a major figure in Spanish poetry, and the publication of *Fields of Castile* cemented that reputation. When the new generation appeared in the 1920's, Machado was momentarily rejected as being old-fashioned. The members of this Generation of 1927—Gerardo Diego, Jorge Guillén, Pedro Salinas, Federico García Lorca, Rafael Alberti—tended to be influenced by international trends and by the poetry of Jiménez, who himself was considered old-fashioned. This generation of Vanguard poets sought to "dehumanize" art, to make it totally art and not life, and indeed to "revolutionize" all artistic values. In poetry the generation struggled to create novel metaphor at any price and emphasized the conceptual at the expense of intuition. In his writing for publication, Machado tried earnestly (but unsuccessfully) to persuade the young Diego, who by chance had followed him at the Institute in Soria, to write a more temporal and human poetry.[5] In private, the old lion was seething that his temporal poetry was being scorned.[6]

Even among the poets of the Generation of 1927, however, it is interesting that many of them later in life made something of a return to Antonio Machado and his manner. The cases of Jorge Guillén and Rafael Alberti are particularly instructive, since when they began, both were quite alienated from Machado's customary manner. In fact, Machado, normally a very generous person, severely censured Guillén for his "conceptual" poetry.[7] As Guillén grew older, his poetry gradually became more human or temporal, and he entitled a later book *A la altura de las circunstancias* after a phrase in *Juan de Mairena.* Moreover, Guillén began to devote serious effort to the creation of gnomic poems of three or four lines which he called *Tréboles,* or "Clovers." These little poems seem clearly in the tradition of Machado's "Proverbs and Songs" in both theme and form, as this example indicates:

> Great poet: gigantic squid
> Who through the water spreads his ink
> Dreaming of being the whole sea.

> *(Gran poeta: gran calamar*
> *Que por el agua arroja tinta*
> *Soñando con ser todo el mar.)*

Rafael Alberti, after an initial burst of neo-popular poetry, in 1929 published two books, *Cal y canto* and *Sobre los ángeles*, either of which was the antithesis of Machado's simple and human manner. In the same period, Alberti was both Baroque in the manner of Góngora and Surrealist in the bravest Vanguard fashion; his poetry was hermetic, complicated, ingenious, and conceptual. After serving in the Civil War, however, he suffered the agony of being exiled from his homeland, and during the years he spent in Argentina his poetry became more simple and human. In 1953, Alberti published his *Coplas de Juan Panadero*, in which his Juan upholds the poetics of Machado's *Juan de Mairena*.

> I say with Juan de Mairena
> "I prefer in verse sparse rhyme,"
> The kind that barely chimes.
>
> *(Digo con Juan de Mairena
> "Prefiero la rima pobre"
> esa que casi no suena.)*

For Alberti this was to come full circle from the charming simplicity of his first book, *Marinero en tierra*, and in his long journey back he was often consciously aware of the spirit of Antonio Machado.

Of all the Generation of 1927, undoubtedly García Lorca was the poet most influenced during the formative years of his career by Machado. According to his contemporary Luis Cernuda, Lorca was so strongly impressed by Machado's *The Land of Alvargonzález* that he went to the trouble of making and producing a dramatic version of it for friends.[8] Machado continued to explore the possibilities of the Andalusian *copla* during Lorca's formative years, but except in conjunction with his ironic metaphysical discourses, he never found the way adequately to utilize the popular manner. Lorca, following Machado's lead, seized upon the popular materials and converted them into the complex artistic and personal literary expression of the *Gypsy Ballads*, the most popular and one of the greatest books of the period.

The agony of the Spanish Civil War heralded a return to the "re-humanization" of art, and in the reevaluation the influence of Antonio Machado has grown steadily, while that of Jiménez has declined. In fact, the respected poet and critic José Luis Cano has spoken firmly of a "return to Antonio Machado, one of the most important phenomena in the evolution of post-war Spanish poetry.[9] Cano mentions as followers of Machado Leopoldo Panero, Luis Rosales, Luis Felipe Vivanco, and Dionisio Ridruejo. All these poets reveal mainly a spiritual kinship, not a direct influence of form and manner. This powerful line from a major poem of Panero's serves well as an example: "Hope is the only truth that man invents" (*La esperanza es la sola verdad que el hombre inventa*). The line sounds hauntingly Machadian, even though it is not a conscious imitation. Cano's list of poets influenced could be easily extended to include the poetess Angela Figuera, whose book *Soria pura* (which inevitably contains a lyric entitled "Antonio Machado") reveals a direct kinship. Moreover, in a general way, the Basque poet Blas de Otero, for many the finest poet of the postwar period, is a spiritual follower of Machado. Otero's favorite theme concerns *living in time* (*Digo vivir*), and he has pursued in his poetry a theme Machado developed mainly in his prose, that of human brotherhood.[10]

Little by little, Machado has become a consecrated historical figure as well as a living influence. The outstanding novelist Camilo José Cela, himself something of a wayfarer, in his book of travels, *Viaje a la Alcarria*, pictures himself as reciting one of Machado's early poems (II).[11] The novelist Juan Goytisolo has called a trilogy of novels *El mañana efímero*, after the title of one of Machado's Castilian poems. In 1965, the poet Félix Grande wrote a poem which is a gloss of two of Machado's well-known lines: "Today you'll seek in vain / Consolation for your pain."[12] As long as our present mood of anguish and alienation endures, undoubtedly Antonio Machado will remain a source of inspiration in Spanish poetry.[13]

On the twentieth anniversary (1959) of Machado's death, in a special edition of the journal *Insula*, a young writer attempted to define Antonio Machado's position among his literary generation, the "grandsons" of the Generation of 98.[14] According to him, while all the members of the Generation of 98 are still respected and living figures, Unamuno, Ortega y Gasset, and Machado are the three most "alive in spirit" for today's youth. And of these three, the one most "unanimously deep-felt" is Antonio Machado, who, in addition to his poetic and human leadership, "awakens a tenderness difficult to explain." Thus many have felt (and found impossible to define) the bond of human sympathy which Machado's work communicates. Despite the tragic political upheavals through which Spain has suffered in this century, this young man can cite some moving words Machado wrote in 1904: "I see poetry as an anvil of constant spiritual activity. . . . All our efforts ought to reach out toward light, toward consciousness."

Finally, it is fitting to return to the three great figures of twentieth-century Spanish poetry, Unamuno, Jiménez, and Antonio Machado. As Jiménez perceptively noted, it was Unamuno who reintroduced the metaphysical themes in Spanish poetry; that is, Unamuno reopened the vital and anguishing problem of human destiny. However, Unamuno still lives most adequately in his extensive prose work. Jiménez and Machado both struggled with the problem of human destiny in their poetry. Very early Jiménez retreated into the confines of his soul and sought to create and project a complete human spirit. His poetry records over many years a succession of victories; during three periods of his life, the poet triumphed in three distinct manners, the aesthetic, the intellectual, and the neo-mystical. Machado classified Jiménez as a "pure" poet, a great compliment which nevertheless implies a significant criticism. The "pure" poet usually suffers from being too ethereal, from being out of touch with humanity. Machado felt that his poetry always had the "impurity" of being human. His was a journey toward otherness, toward the reality of human love and a loving God. Three times he sallied forth on his poetic journey, and after every effort in a sense he fell back defeated. It is not an idle comparison to note that Cervantes' Don Quixote suffered the same fate of going forth in hope and returning in defeat. Like his illustrious forebear, Antonio Machado in his defeats bequeathed to us the record of a "good man" who *lived* in time and memory. His spirit lives on in most adequate focus there in the Sorian highlands where the white road winds along the Duero River, but it has also expanded outward in widening circles to pervade Spanish literature and life.

Notes and References

Chapter One

1. There is a fine discussion of this period in the opening chapters of Luis Granjel's *Panorama de la generación del 98* (Madrid, 1959).
2. The author enjoyed a long interview with Señor Joaquín Malo de Molina in July, 1968, in Madrid.
3. Machado recalled this episode in *Obras, poesía y prosa* (Buenos Aires, 1964), p. 508. Hereafter we shall cite this edition as *Works*.
4. *Works*, p. 507. See also, *Works*, p. 720.
5. See Antonio Jiménez Landi, *Don Francisco Giner de los Ríos y la Institución Libre de Enseñanza* (New York, 1959).
6. Juan López-Morillas' *El krausismo español* is the standard study of this philosophy.
7. These sketches have been republished by Aurora de Albornoz, *La prehistoria de Antonio Machado* (Río Piedras, Puerto Rico, 1961).
8. See Geoffrey Ribbans, "Unamuno and Antonio Machado," *Bulletin of Hispanic Studies*, 91-92 (1957), 180-201. Also, Aurora de Albornoz, *La presencia de Unamuno en Antonio Machado* (Madrid, 1968).
9. This letter is quoted by Ribbans in the article just cited.
10. *Works*, pp. 765-67.
11. Eduardo Luis del Palacio, "Apuntes para una semblanza de Antonio Machado, expositor y catedrático," *Poesía española* (Madrid), 69 (April, 1958), 8-12.
12. See Heliodoro Carpintero, "Soria en la vida y en la obra de Antonio Machado," *Escorial*, XII (July, 1943), 111-27.
13. See Antonio Obregón, "Machado en Baeza," *ABC* (Madrid), Oct. 10, 1963, and Francisco Escolano, "Antonio Machado en Baeza," *El Español* (Madrid), Nov. 14, 1942, p. 3, for more details on this period.

14. *Works*, p. 904.
15. *Ibid.*, p. 917.
16. *Ibid.*, pp. 913-25. There are four important letters.
17. M. Cardenal de Iracheta, "Crónica de don Antonio y sus amigos en Segovia," *Cuadernos hispanoamericanos* (Madrid), XI-XII (1949), 301-6.
18. *Works*, pp. 814-19.
19. Justina Ruiz de Conde, *Antonio Machado y Guiomar* (Madrid, 1964), pp. 17ff.
20. *Insula*, 158 (1960), 5.
21. *Works*, pp. 842-57.
22. *Works*, pp. 865-94.
23. This lady is Doña María de Souto, who now lives in Oak Ridge, Tennessee.
24. The details of Machado's last days are well summarized in Gabrial Pradal-Rodríguez, "Antonio Machado: vida y obra," *Revista hispánica moderna*, XV (1949), 1-6.

Chapter Two

1. Ramón de Zubiría, *La poesía de Antonio Machado* (Madrid, 1955).
2. José M. Valverde, "Evolución del sentido espiritual de la obra de Antonio Machado," *Cuadernos hispanoamericanos,* XI-XII (1949), 399-414.
3. Ricardo Gullón, *Conversaciones con Juan Ramón Jiménez* (Madrid, 1958), p. 57.
4. Geoffrey Ribbans, "Antonio Machado's *Soledades* (1903): A Critical Study," *Hispanic Review*, XXX (1962), 194-215.
5. See Rafael Lapesa, "Bécquer, Rosalía y Machado," *Insula*, 100-101 (1954), 6.
6. The poems in Machado's *Works* are numbered consecutively with Roman numerals. We shall identify poems cited by these numbers throughout this book.
7. *Works*, p. 498.
8. Geoffrey Ribbans, "La influencia de Verlaine en Antonio Machado," *Cuadernos hispanoamericanos,* 91-92 (19-57), 180-201.
9. *Works*, p. 48.
10. *Ibid.*, pp. 46-47.
11. *Ibid.*, pp. 31-32.

12. Machado inexplicably put the poem in the section before "Galerías."
13. R. A. Molina, " 'Anoche cuando dormía,' " *Insula*, 158 (1960), 1-2.
14. *Works*, p. 563.
15. Ricardo Gullón, p. 106.
16. *Works*, p. 712.
17. *Ibid.*, p. 713.

Chapter Three

1. See Luis Granjel, *Panorama de la generación del 98* (Madrid, 1959), Chapter 2.
2. Unamuno confessed this same failure. See Miguel de Unamuno, *Sus mejores páginas*, ed. Philip Metzidakis (Englewood Cliffs, New Jersey, 1966), p. 86.
3. Prologue to *Fields of Castile, Works*, p. 7.
4. See especially two articles by Helen F. Grant, *"La tierra de Alvargonzález,"* *Celtiberia* (Soria), V (1953), 57-90, and "Antonio Machado and *La tierra de Alvargonzález,"* *Atlante* (London), II (1954), 139-58. Also Allen W. Phillips, *"La tierra de Alvargonzález: verso y prosa,"* *Nueva revista de filología hispánica*, IX (1953), 129-48.
5. José M. Valverde, "Evolución del sentido . . . ," *Cuadernos hispanoamericanos*, XI-XII (1949), 399-414.
6. *Works*, p. 903.
7. See Luis Felipe Vivanco, "Comentario a unos pocos poemas de Antonio Machado," *Cuadernos hispanoamericanos*, XI-XII (1949), 541-65.

Chapter Four

1. *Works*, p. 464.
2. *Works*, p. 322.
3. We lack the space to differentiate between these *personae*, and when we use their names we only mean "Machado" seeking a bit of distance from which to view himself and others.
4. See Segundo Serrano Poncela, *Del Romancero a Machado* (Caracas, 1962), pp. 173-84.
5. *Works*, pp. 197-209.
6. *Ibid.*, pp. 252-69.
7. Every student of Machado's ideas is indebted to the out-

standing article by Antonio Sánchez Barbudo, "El pensamiento de Antonio Machado en relación con su poesía," in *Estudios sobre Unamuno y Machado* (Madrid, 1959). See also the book by Pablo A. Cobos, *Humor y pensamiento de Antonio Machado* (Madrid, 1963).

8. See the long article by Luis Rosales, "Muerte y resurrección de Antonio Machado," *Cuadernos hispanoamericanos*, XI-XII (1949), 435-79.

9. Machado continued to write of Guiomar even during the Civil War. In one sonnet, found among Manuel's papers later, he even uses her real name (Pilar), slightly disguised poetically. See *Works*, p. 759.

10. Machado develops the idea of fraternal love in the prose of *Juan de Mairena.*

Chapter Five

1. *Works*, pp. 502-3.
2. *Ibid.*, p. 405.
3. *Ibid.*, p. 391.
4. *Ibid.*, p. 351.
5. *Ibid.*, pp. 429-32. See Carlos Beceiro's article, "Una fase de Juan de Mairena," *Insula*, 158 (1960), 13, 15.
6. *Works*, pp. 433-34.
7. *Ibid.*, p. 470.
8. *Ibid.*, p. 391.
9. *Ibid.*, pp. 398-99.
10. *Ibid.*, p. 585.
11. *Ibid.*, pp. 483-84.
12. *Ibid.*, p. 512.
13. *Ibid.*, p. 449.
14. *Ibid.*, p. 512.
15. *Ibid.*, pp. 511-12.
16. *Ibid.*, p. 483.
17. *Ibid.*, pp. 467ff.
18. There are many references to Communism, Marx, Russia, Dostoevsky, etc. His article "On Russian Literature" (*Works*, pp. 814-19) indicates the depth of his Russian studies.
19. *Works*, pp. 547-48.
20. *Ibid.*, pp. 411ff.
21. *Ibid.*, p. 423.
22. *Ibid.*, p. 453.

23. *Ibid.*, pp. 587-88.
24. Luis Cernuda, *Estudios sobre poesía española contemporánea* (Madrid, 1957), p. 106.

Chapter Six

1. Manuel H. Guerra's *El teatro de Manuel y Antonio Machado* (Madrid, 1966), contains a wealth of details, though relatively limited criticism, of the Machado theater.
2. Miguel Pérez Ferrero, *Vida de Antonio Machado y Manuel*, pp. 159-60.
3. See Manuel H. Guerra, pp. 64ff.
4. Angel Valbuena Prat, *Historia general de las literaturas hispánicas*, VI (Barcelona, 1967), p. 206.
5. See the letter quoted in Guerra, pp. 188-89.
6. Guerra (pp. 13ff.) presents helpful data on the condition of the theater.
7. Pérez Ferrero, p. 164.
8. Guerra, p. 184.
9. Valbuena Prat, *Historia del teatro español* (Barcelona, 1956), p. 618.
10. Quoted in Pérez Ferrero, p. 165.
11. *Works*, pp. 382-83.
12. Gabriel Pradal-Rodríguez, "Antonio Machado: vida y obra," *Revista hispánica moderna*, I-IV (1949), 65.
13. *Works*, pp. 411ff.
14. See Concha Espina, *De Antonio Machado a su grande y secreto amor*, p. 56.
15. *Ibid.*, pp. 97-98.
16. *Works*, p. 413.

Chapter Seven

1. Ricardo Gullón, *Conversaciones con Juan Ramón Jiménez*, p. 106.
2. *Works*, p. 712.
3. *Ibid.*, p. 713.
4. *Ibid.*, p. 315.
5. *Ibid.*, pp. 810-11, 931-32.
6. Antonio's private correspondence with Guiomar contains many negative opinions that he preferred not to publish.
7. *Works*, p. 835.

8. Luis Cernuda, *Estudios sobre poesía española contemporánea*, p. 114

9. José Luis Cano, *Antología de la nueva poesía española* (Madrid, 1963), p. 14.

10. Of course Otero was also influenced by his fellow Basque, Unamuno.

11. Camilo José Cela, *Viaje a la Alcarria* (Boston, 1962), pp. 36-37.

12. Félix Grande, *Música amenazada* (Barcelona, 1966), pp. 20-21.

13. Machado's influence in Hispanic America has apparently been very general, while that of Jiménez and Lorca has been specific and strong. An interesting exception is the Argentine Francisco Romero's article on Juan de Mairena. See Anderson-Imbert and Florit's *Literatura hispanoamericana* (New York, 1960), pp. 644-47.

14. José R. Marra López, "La juventud ante Machado," *Insula*, 158 (1960), 6.

Selected Bibliography

PRIMARY SOURCES

Soledades (Madrid: A. Alvarez, 1903).
Soledades, galerías y otros poemas (Madrid: Pueyo, 1907).
Campos de Castilla (Madrid: Renacimiento, 1912).
Poesías completas (Madrid: Fortanet, 1917).
De un cancionero apócrifo (Madrid: Revista de Occidente, 1926).
Poesías completas (Madrid: Espasa-Calpe, 1928, 1933, 1936, 1941, 1946, 1958, 1962, etc.).
Nuevas canciones (Madrid: Mundo Latino, 1924).
Poesías completas (Buenos Aires: Losada, 1943, 1946, 1958, 1962, etc.). This inexpensive text contains all of Machado's essential poetry.
Juan de Mairena, Sentencias, donaires, apuntes y recuerdos de un profesor apócrifo (Madrid: Espasa-Calpe, 1936).
La guerra (Madrid: Espasa-Calpe, 1937).
Las adelfas y El hombre que murió en la guerra (Buenos Aires: Espasa-Calpe, 1947).
Obras completas de Manuel y Antonio Machado (Madrid: Editorial Plenitud, 1947. Fourth edition, 1957). Contains the Machados' drama also, except for *El hombre que murió en la guerra.*
Poesie di Antonio Machado, ed. di Oreste Macrí (Milan: Casa Editrice Il Balcone, 1959). This edition has the textual variants of his poems.
Obras, poesía y prosa (Buenos Aires: Losada, 1964).

SECONDARY SOURCES

Albornoz, Aurora de. *La prehistoria de Antonio Machado* (Río Piedras, Puerto Rico: Ediciones La Torre, 1961). Contains Machado's satirical articles.

—————. *La presencia de Unamuno en Machado* (Madrid: Ed. Gredos, 1968). A study which goes beyond the specific influences of Unamuno.

Alonso, Dámaso. *Poetas españoles contemporáneos* (Madrid: Gredos, 1952).

—————. *Cuatro poetas españoles* (Madrid: Gredos, 1961). Alonso's two books have articles on Machado which demonstrate their author's unusual capacity as critic and poet.

Barnstone, Willis. *Eighty Poems of Antonio Machado* (New York: Las Américas, 1959). Somewhat literal versions of selected poems.

Bousoño, Carlos. *Teoría de la expresión poética* (Madrid: Gredos, 1962). Has a fine technical study of Machado's symbolism.

Cernuda, Luis. *Estudios sobre poesía española contemporánea* (Madrid: Guadarrama, 1958). An appreciative (but personal) chapter on Machado.

Cobos, Pablo A. *Humor y pensamiento en la metafísica poética de Antonio Machado* (Madrid: Insula, 1963). An important study of Machado's third period.

Cuadernos hispanoamericanos (Madrid), XI-XII (1949). An entire issue devoted to articles on Machado.

Espina, Concha. *De Antonio Machado a su grande y secreto amor* (Madrid: Gráficas Reunidas, 1950). Contains Machado's revealing letters to Guiomar.

Granjel, Luis. *Panorama de la generación del 98* (Madrid: Guadarrama, 1959). Excellent study of Machado's Generation of 98, according to essential themes, including texts from authors discussed.

Guerra, Manuel H. *El teatro de Manuel y Antonio Machado* (Madrid: Ed. Mediterráneo, 1966). A wealth of details on the Machados' theater, including critics' articles at time of premieres.

Gullón, Ricardo. *Las galerías secretas de Antonio Machado* (Madrid: Taurus, 1958). An example of the criticism of Gullón, who has written a number of articles on the poet.

Insula (Madrid), 158 (1960). An issue devoted to articles on Machado.

Laín Entralgo, Pedro. *La generación del 98* (Madrid: Ed. Diana,

1945). Another excellent study of the Generation, according to themes.

Machado, José. *Últimas soledades del poeta Antonio Machado* (Santiago de Chile, Typed Edition, 1958). Personal reminiscences of the poet's brother.

McVan, Alice Jane. *Antonio Machado* (New York: The Hispanic Society, 1959). Important supplementary biographical details and an anthology of translations of poetry.

Montserrat, Santiago. *Antonio Machado, poeta y filósofo* (Córdoba, Argentina: Universidad Nacional, 1960).

Orozco Díaz, Emilio. *Antonio Machado en el camino* (Granada: Univ. de Granada, 1961).

Peers, E. Allison. *Antonio Machado* (Oxford: Clarendon Press, 1940). A brief study emphasizing the Machado of Castilian theme.

Pérez Ferrero, M. *Vida de Antonio Machado y Manuel* (Madrid: Artes Gráficas, 1947). Up to now, the standard biography.

Pradal-Rodríguez, Gabriel. "Antonio Machado: vida y obra," *Revista hispánica moderna*, I-IV (1949), 1-98, 153-247. A biography and critical study.

Ruiz de Conde, Justina. *Antonio Machado y Guiomar* (Madrid: Insula, 1964). A collection of previously published articles.

Sánchez Barbudo, Antonio. *Estudios sobre Unamuno y Machado* (Madrid: Guadarrama, 1959). A penetrating study of Machado's philosophical ideas (and the influences upon them) in relation to his poetry.

—————. *Los poemas de Antonio Machado* (Barcelona: Ed. Lumen, 1967). A detailed study of Machado's poems, one by one.

Serrano Poncela, Segundo. *Antonio Machado, su mundo y su obra* (Buenos Aires: Losada, 1954). A competent study of Machado's inner world and ideas.

Trend, J. B. *Antonio Machado* (Oxford: Dolphin Book Co., 1953). A brief study emphasizing Machado's Castilian period.

Zubiría, Ramón de. *La poesía de Antonio Machado* (Madrid: Ed. Gredos, 1955). An excellent study of Machado's poetry according to the essential themes of time and memory.

Index

(Machado's works are listed under the Spanish title)

Adelfas, Las (*Bitter Oleander*), 155ff., 152, 163
Agamemnon, 131
Alarcón, Pedro, 18
Alberti, Rafael, 170, 171
Almazán, Adolfo, 31
Alonso, Dámaso, Preface
Aristotle, 30, 132, 134, 136
Arranz, Fernando, 34
Ayuso, Manuel, 27
Azorín (José Martínez Ruiz), 31, 32, 47, 76, 77, 78, 83, 93, 129, 153

Baeza, 26, 29ff., 97, 102
Barnstone, Willis, Preface
Baroja, Pío, 47, 77, 78, 83, 129
Barral, Emiliano, 35
Bécquer, Gustavo Adolfo, 18, 20, 24, 45-46, 56, 70, 75, 131, 164, 166
Bédier, 28
Benavente, Jacinto, 149, 150
Berceo, Gonzalo de, 79, 95
Bergson, 28, 30, 101-2, 136

Cain-Abel theme, 32, 88
Calderón de la Barca, Pedro, 23, 131, 152
Calvo, Ricardo, 23, 25, 39, 145, 162
Campoamor, Ramón de, 18, 75, 164
Campos de Castilla (*Fields of Castile*), 28, 29, 33, 43, 76-103, 104, 106, 127, 142, 144, 166, 169
Cano, José Luis, 171, 172

Cantares (*Songs*), 25, 44
Capek, 150
Caricatura, La (journal), 23
Carlyle, 137
Casona, Alejandro, 163
Castilian theme, 78 ff.
Castro, Rosalía de, 18, 24
Cela, Camilo José, 172
Cernuda, Luis, 144
Cervantes, Miguel de, 25, 27, 50, 130, 140, 173
Cobos, Pablo de A., Preface
copla, 33, 76, 106, 111, 127, 128, 136
Corral, Ignacio, 35
Cuadernos hispanoamericanos (journal), 42

Darío, Rubén, 18, 19, 24, 32, 46, 79, 89, 95, 148, 164, 165
Descartes, 130, 136
Desdichas de la Fortuna, o Julianillo Valcárcel (*The Workings of Fate*), 38, 151ff., 162
De un cancionero apócrifo (*From an Apocryphal Songbook*), 38, 105, 110ff., 165
Dickinson, Emily, 49, 165
Diego, Gerardo, 170
Dostoevsky, 137, 138, 169
Duero River, 26, 31, 42, 80, 81, 82, 89, 103, 173
Duquesa de Benamejí, La (*The Duchess of Benamejí*), 159ff.

Echegaray, José, 18, 23, 39, 149
Electra (journal), 44

Elogios (Poems of praise), 92ff., 166

Emerson, 137

Espina, Concha, 36

Espronceda, José de, 131

"Essential heterogeneity of being," 110, 113, 135, 139, 165

Existentialism, 73, 75, 98, 169

Falla, Manuel de, 31

Feuerbach, 135

Figuera, Angela, 172

Freud, 49, 70, 114, 139, 155, 156

Frost, Robert, 80, 103

Ganivet, Angel, 18, 32

García Lorca, Federico, 31, 36, 92, 145, 151, 164, 171

Generation of 98, 18, 19, 30, 76-77, 80, 82, 129, 130, 134, 144, 149, 163, 166, 172

Giner, Francisco, 21, 32, 93, 129, 137, 141

God, 39, 68, 84, 105, 108, 121-23, 125, 134, 136, 167, 169

Gómez Carillo, Enrique, 24

Góngora, Luis de, 47, 92

Goytisolo, Juan, 172

Grande, Félix, 172

Granjel, Luis, 77

Grau, Jacinto, 150, 153

Guillén, Jorge, 170

Guiomar, 36ff., 39, 40, 41, 113, 114-21, 147, 155, 157, 158, 159, 160

Gullón, Ricardo, 43

Hegel, 30

Heidegger, 73, 130

Heraclitus, 61, 130, 140

Hombre que murió en la guerra, El (*The Man Who Died in the War*), 160ff.

Hora de España (journal), 41

Institución Libre de Enseñanza

(Free Institute), 18, 21-22, 39, 141

Insula (journal), 42, 172

Izquierdo, Leonor, 27ff., 76, 95ff.

Jesus, 32, 107, 121, 134, 135, 136

Jiménez, Juan Ramón, 24, 29, 33, 44, 45, 46, 50, 75, 77, 92, 95, 164, 165, 167, 168, 170, 171, 173

Johnson, Jack, 131

Joyce, James, 40

Juan de Mairena (book), 39, 40, 99, 128ff., 153, 155, 160, 161, 162, 164, 165, 170, 171

Juan de Mañara, 153ff., 162, 163

Kant, 30, 130, 136, 143

Kierkegaard, 17, 169

Krausismo (krausism), 22, 27, 137, 141

Leibnitz, 30, 111

Lola se va a los puertos, La (*La Lola Goes Off to Sea*), 38, 156ff., 162

Loyola, Ignatius de, 87

McVan, Alice Jane, Preface

Machado, Joaquín, 20, 147

Machado, José, 20, 42

Machado, Manuel, 20, 22, 23, 25, 36, 38, 41, 42, 145ff., 164, 165

Machado Alvarez, Antonio (father), 19, 22

Machado Núñez, Antonio (grandfather), 19-21

Madrid (journal), 41

Maeztu, Ramiro de, 77, 83

Mairena, Juan de (*persona*), 36, 114, 124, 126, 147, 171

Malo de Molina, Joaquín, 20, 30

Manrique, Jorge, 65-66, 68, 100, 165

Marquina, Eduardo, 150, 153

Martín, Abel (*persona*), 36, 38, 105, 111ff., 132, 147

Martínez Sierra, Gregorio, 28, 153
Marx, Karl, 130, 138
Membrives, Lola, 157, 158
Meneses, Jorge (persona), 105, 126-27
Modernismo (Modernism), 19, 25, 60, 79, 148, 167
Moreas, Jean, 24

Nietzsche, 17, 30, 130, 136, 137
Nuevas canciones (New Songs), 33, 43, 76, 109
Numancia, 27
Núñez de Arce, Gaspar, 18, 75, 164

Ortega y Gasset, José, 30, 31, 32, 35, 94-95, 135, 137, 144
Otero, Blas de, 172
Otero, Julián, 35
Otherness, 121

Palacio, José María, 27, 97
Palacio Valdés, Armando, 18
Panero, Leopoldo, 172
Paradas, Enrique, 22, 23
Peers, E. Allison, 43
Pereda, José María, 18
Pérez Ferrero, Miguel, Preface, 36, 148
Pérez Galdós, Benito, 18
Petrarch, 100
Pirandello, 150, 161
Plato, 30, 39, 112, 130, 133
Poe, Edgar A., 47
Poesías completas (Complete Poems), 33, 44, 76, 168
Prima Fernanda, La (Cousin Fernanda), 158ff., 162
Proust, 40
"Proverbs and Songs," 43, 76, 104, 105-10, 127
Pueyo, Gregorio, 35

Quintanilla, Mariano, 35

Revista de Occidente, La (journal), 35

Ribbans, Geoffrey, 47
Ridruejo, Dionisio, 172
Rosales, Luis, 172
Royal Spanish Academy, 39-40, 42
Ruiz de Conde, Justina, 36
Ruiz de Machado, Doña Ana (mother), 20, 21, 29, 42

St. John of the Cross, 72, 87
St. Theresa, 72
Salinas, Pedro, 170
Sánchez Barbudo, Preface
Sanz del Río, Julián, 22
Scheler, 135
Schleiermacher, 135
Schopenhauer, 17, 30, 130
Segovia, 33ff., 118, 145
Sem Tob, 106
Seville, 20, 46, 61, 78
Shakespeare, 20, 49, 130
Socrates, 39, 129, 130, 132
Soledades (Solitudes), 25, 43-75, 77, 79, 104, 123, 127, 165, 166, 168, 169
Soria, 26ff., 42, 85ff., 173
Symbolism, 19, 24, 46, 71, 75, 148

Tertulia (literary gathering), 30, 35, 145
Thoreau, 137
Tierra de Alvargonzález, La (The Land of Alvargonzález), 28, 31, 88-92
Tirso de Molina, 146, 151, 153
Tolstoy, 36, 41, 130, 137, 138
Torres, Cristóbal, 31
Trend, J.B., 43

Unamuno, Miguel de, 18, 25, 26, 29, 30, 31, 32, 33, 38, 77, 78, 83, 88, 92-93, 101, 129, 131, 134, 135, 137, 141, 142, 144, 149, 153, 164, 172, 173

Valbuena Prat, Angel, 144, 146, 152

Valcarce, Xavier, 32, 95
Valderrama, Pilar de (Guiomar), 37ff.
Valera, Juan, 18
Valle-Inclán, Ramón del, 25, 32, 41, 131, 149, 153
Valverde, José María, 91
Vega, Garcilaso de la, 92, 97
Vega, Lope de, 131, 146, 152
Velázquez, Diego de, 135

Verlaine, 24, 26, 46-47, 61, 64
Vigodksy, David, 41
Villalba, Padre, 35
Vivanco, Luis Felipe, 172

Wilde, Oscar, 24

Zayas, Antonio de, 23
Zembrano, Blas, 34
Zorrilla, José, 92, 131, 153, 164
Zubiría, Ramón de, 43